Daddy's Hugs

Charlotte Russell Johnson

The author of
A Journey to Hell and Back

Copyright © 2003 Charlotte Johnson
A production of
Reaching Beyond, Inc.
P. O. Box 12364
Columbus, GA 31917-2364
(706) 221-9053

World rights reserved. No part of this publication may be stored in a retrieval system, transmitted, or reproduced in any way, including but not limited to photocopy, photograph, magnetic or other record, without prior agreement and written permission of the author.

Daddy's Hugs

What exactly is it that you expect of me?
Please define it for me?
Is it something that I could never be?
Is it something that I don't know how to be?

A daughter to my mother?
Is that what you expect me to be?
That's a bit confusing to me...
She's trying to be something she could never be...
A Mommy and a Daddy to me...
So what is it that you expect me to rise above?
I had no Daddy's hugs, no Daddy's kisses, and no Daddy's love...

A mother to my child?
Why would you expect that of me?
I've got my own issues, can't you see?
There is still a hole inside of me...
No one has defined a man's love for me...
I had no Daddy's hugs, no Daddy's kisses, and no Daddy's love...

A father to my daughter?
Did you really expect that of me?
Coddle her, hold her, reassure her...
Is that what you really expected from me?
Fondle her, molest her, and threaten her...
That's what it meant to me...
Who was my example supposed to be?
I had no Daddy's hugs, no Daddy's kisses, and no Daddy's love...

A father to my Son?
How could you expect that of me?
That's the laughing one...
I still wonder where "Real Men" come from...
Who was supposed to teach that to me?
I had no Daddy's hugs, no Daddy's kisses, and no Daddy's love...

A son to my mother?
Is that what you expect from me?
Where was I supposed to learn that from?
Was she the one I was supposed to get my masculinity from?
She confused me with all her sensitivity...
My Daddy she could never be...
Who was the example to me?
I had no Daddy's hugs, no Daddy's kisses, and no Daddy's love...

A wife to my husband?
Is that something you really expected of me?
Honor him, respect him, and support him?
What's that supposed to mean to me?
I have only seen strong independent women...
I don't have that identity...
Who was supposed to teach that to me?
I had no Daddy's hugs, no Daddy's kisses, and no Daddy's love...

A husband to my wife?
Is that something you really expected of me?
Respect her, protect her, and be faithful to her...
What's that supposed to mean to me?
Neglect her, beat her, and cheat on her...
That's what it means to me...
I don't have that identity...
Who was supposed to teach that to me?
I had no Daddy's hugs, no Daddy's kisses, and no Daddy's love...

Faithful and true?
You must be kidding me.
Who was my example supposed to be?
Who was committed to me?
He said he was coming back...
Who was supposed to pick up the slack?
I had no Daddy's hugs, no Daddy's kisses, and no Daddy's love...

A respectable member of society?
Now please define that for me.
All I know is what I see on TV...
Crime, murder, hatred, and drugs are all around me...
Now you tell me not believe what I see?
You must be kidding me...
It's my environment that I see...
Who was supposed to provide for me?
I had no Daddy's hugs, no Daddy's kisses, and no Daddy's love...

An example for me?
How can this be?
Please explain that to me?
I had no Daddy's hugs, no Daddy's kisses, and no Daddy's love...
You say there is one who knows how to love me?
How can He love a failure like me?
He loves me so much that He died for me?
You mean there is one who cares about me?
He'll give me Daddy's hugs, Daddy's kisses, and Daddy's love...

DEDICATION

This book is dedicated to the memory of:
Herman Russell Jr.

July 10, 1937 - July 18, 1962

My heart still bleeds for you.

Special thanks to all the fathers who stuck around to provide a positive example for your children.

Very special thanks to
Mr. Charlie C. Walker for filling some of the holes in my life.

Expectations

Preface 11

Introduction 13

The Paintbrush 15

The Myths, the Lies 17

My Scars 25

A Daughter to my Mother 39

A Mother to my Child 47

A Father to my Daughter 59

A Father to my Son 77

A Son to my Mother 85

A Wife to my Husband 99

A Husband to my Wife 111

Faithful and True 117

A Respectable Member
of Society 127

An Example for Me 137

The Charge 149

Father Help Me 157

From the Heart of Charlotte 161

Prologue 169

Preface

Children, obey your parents in the Lord, for this is right.

Throughout this book, you will see pictures of various fathers with their children. Some of the most precious fatherly interactions that I have observed have been between my brother-in-law and his children. He has a very special relationship with each of his children. There are a number of pictures of my uncle, Albert Huntley. He's a Daddy.

Since my last book, my sister Crystal gave birth to another son. She now has six children, three boys and three girls. She gave each of the girls a part of my name. References will be made to these children throughout the book.

My personal pains because of my father's absence and the pain that I have seen in others have triggered this book. My father was taken from my life without his consent. He never walked away from his fatherly responsibility, yet the pain is still the same. It left deep wounds in my life. Out of necessity, this book will refer to some of the incidents related in *A Journey to Hell and Back*.

This book is not an attack on fathers, but rather an exhalation for them to be the king of the house that God created them to be. Thus, we have *Daddy's Hugs*.

Introduction
From the Heart of Earline

The text's major premise is that the role of fathers is essential to promote healthy child development and appropriate role modeling. The book exhorts the role of fatherhood in the lives of children. Daddy's Hugs offers striking commentary on the plight of fatherless children. Fathers are portrayed as more than financial breadwinners. Instead, they are depicted as essential emotional caregivers. The book praises and provides examples of fathers who take an active role in parenting. There is an excellent balance of positive, negative, and neutral fathering role models. The humorous vignettes make this book an easy read. The book is able to stray away from the common mistake of male bashing. The devaluation of the role of fathers and their inadequate preparation for this role is explored in-depth. Women are not viewed as passive victims to be exploited by males, but as active participants in child rearing and parenting.

It reveals groundbreaking insight into the importance of male role models to prepare males for life and women for mate selection. It is one of the most radical paradigm shifts in child development, since Dr. Benjamin Spock's *Baby and Child Care*. This book is excellent for mothers, fathers, children, potential parents and partners, as well as those who will work with individuals, families, or are in need of a good laugh.

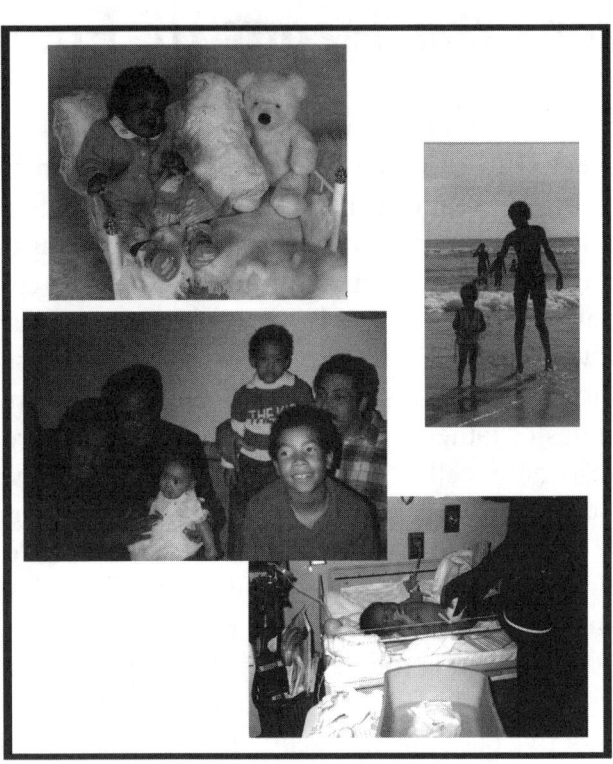

The Paintbrush

I keep my paintbrush with me,
Wherever I may go,
In case, I need to cover up,
So the real me doesn't show.

I'm afraid to show you me,
Afraid of what you'll do.
You just might laugh or say mean things,
I'm afraid that I might lose you.

I'd like to remove my paint coats,
To show you the real true me.
But I want you to try and understand,
I need you to like what you see.

So if you will be patient and close your eyes,
I'll strip off my coats real slow.
Please understand how much it hurts,
To let the real me show.

Now my paint coats are all stripped off,
I feel naked, bare, and cold.
If you still love me,
With all that you see,

You're my friend,
As pure as gold.

I need to keep my paint though,
And hold it in my hand,
Someone might not understand.

So, please protect me my dear friend,
And thanks for loving me true.
But please let me keep my paint brush with me,
Until I love me too….

Original Author Unknown

The Myths, the Lies

False humility is really self-righteousness.
Earline L. Hall

**My son, obey your father's commands, and don't neglect your mother's teaching.
Proverbs 6:20**

My son, Herman, was "special before his birth." He was always very active, rough, adventurous, or shall we just say, "all boy." In *A Journey to Hell and Back*, I shared several of his escapades, and I am going to share yet another. Actually, I could write a book about his numerous adventures.

During his early years, it was necessary for us to make several trips to the hospital emergency room. He was always getting into something. When he was around four years old, I noticed that his pinkie finger was crooked on his right hand. It was also slightly swollen. This was obviously not the normal condition of his finger. As a concerned and dutiful mother, I began to question him.

"Herman what happened to your finger?"
"Oh, I hurt it the other day playing football."
"Who were you playing with?"
"Buck Daddy and Uncle Teddy."
"Tell me what happened."

"When I caught the ball, my finger went back."

"Where was I when this happened? I don't remember hearing you cry."

He responded simply, "You were in the house but I didn't cry."

"You didn't cry! Well, did it hurt?"

"Yes! But I didn't cry."

"Why?"

"They said, real men don't cry."

We took Herman to the hospital emergency room. The x-rays revealed that the bones of his broken finger had begun to grow back together in the deformed pattern. If we wanted the finger to heal correctly, the bone would have to be broken and reset. Like a "Real Man," he didn't cry, but the damage remained. How many times has this scenario been repeated with different boys and different circumstances? They didn't cry but an invisible pain or injury remained.

Who invented this myth? Who invented this lie? Who said real men don't cry? Even our Lord and Savior Jesus Christ cried. As He stood near the tomb of His dear friend Lazarus, our Savior began to weep. He knew that He held the power to raise Lazarus from the dead. However, He wept. He displayed for us a normal reaction to pain and suffering. And yes, a real man cried.

How easy it is for us to disregard the examples and teachings of Jesus, and continue with Pharisaical traditions. If only we could learn to let love and grace richly abound. The results would exceed our greatest expectations. Real love transcends rigid traditions.

Now let your unfailing love comfort me, just as you promised me, your servant. Psalms 119:76 NLT

My brother-in-law is usually seen with at least two babies in his arms, sometimes three. He's not concerned about rigid traditions or stereotypes. He's more concerned about showering his children with Daddy's hugs, Daddy's kisses, and Daddy's love. Kayla will share Daddy's hugs, Daddy's kisses, and Daddy's love. However, after a few minutes, she wants all the hugs, kisses, and love for herself. She fights Cameron for the position in their Daddy's arms. Cameron allows her to have her way. He refuses to hit his younger sister. Cameron is four years older than Kayla. She's agreeable to sharing with three month old Nicholas, at least until he's old enough to fight.

We live in a society that has taught men that it is not masculine to cry, be tender, or openly express their feelings. When men hurt, they are often expected to keep their pain hidden inside. What happens to the pain that goes unexpressed or unattended? Does the pain go away? On the other hand, does it find ventilation in other ways? Does this pain manifest in rage, anger, rape, molestation, adultery, fornication, drunkenness, crime, addiction, violence, murder, and overall degradation of our society?

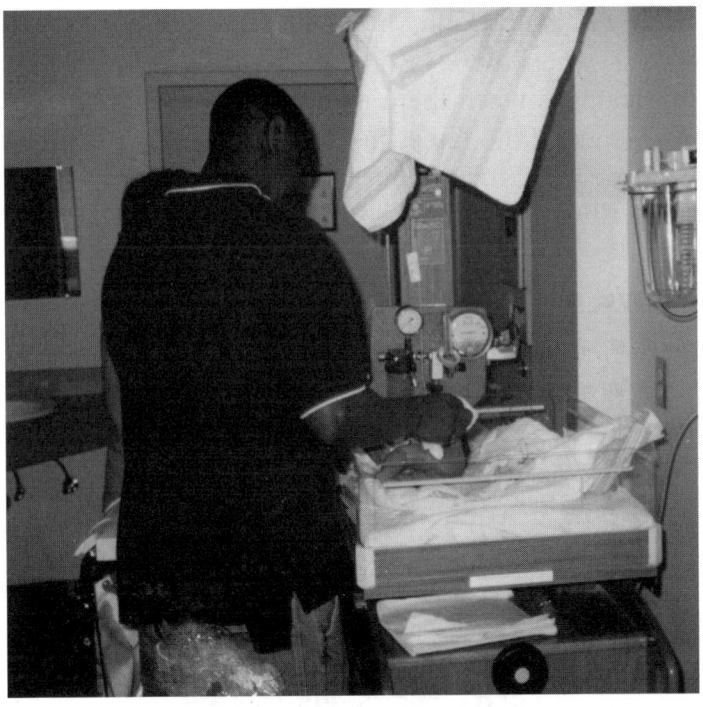

How do you define a *Real Man*? Where does a man learn to be a *Real Man*? What happens when there is no positive male role model in the home? Where does a woman learn how to relate to a man? Where does she get her inner identity? Where does she get her perceptions or expectations of *Real Men*? The answers or lack of answers to these questions triggers my next question. Is the answer found in one simple yet sweet word, Daddy? Then my next question comes to mind. What happens when there is no *Real Man* in the home? What happens when there is no Daddy in the home? I don't mean what happens when there is no father in the home. I mean what happens when there is no Daddy in the home. Has the absence of the father in the home, in fact contributed to the degradation of our society, the simple lack of Daddy's hugs, Daddy's kisses, and Daddy's love?

**We need four hugs a day for survival.
We need eight hugs a day for maintenance.
We need 12 hugs a day for growth.**
—Virginia Satir, Family Therapist

And now a word to you fathers. Don't make your children angry by the way you treat them. Rather, bring them up with the discipline and instruction approved by the Lord. Ephesians 6:4 NLT

While on tour with *A Journey to Hell and Back* in Miami, Florida, I had the opportunity to meet a wonderful brother and his wife. They showed me amazing kindness and godly love. However, what stands out in my mind about him is a term that he continuously used. He constantly referred to our Lord and Savior as "My Daddy." This term of endearment adequately defines one of His most loving roles. He is a *Real Man,* a real Daddy.

The true father (Daddy) delights in his children. Fathers have a wonderful opportunity to teach, model, and mentor their children, displaying for them the heart and character of our heavenly Father. Probably one of the greatest needs among children is to develop a healthy and proper self-respect based on their personal accomplishments, achievements, and successes. This need can only be met by helping the children apply their own abilities and skills in accomplishing or achieving their own dreams.

At three years old, Kim could be seen peering out the upstairs bedroom of her home, in the late hours of the night. When you yelled to her, "Get out of that window and go to bed," she responded adamantly.

The answer was always the same. "I'm waiting for my Daddy."

Each night she returned to her post at the window. She refused to go to sleep until she knew that Daddy was safely home. Whenever you looked up at the window, there was a small face leaning near the window of the dark room. She never went to sleep, until, she was sure that Daddy made it home.

All through the Bible, we see fathers displaying great love and caring for their families, e.g. Abraham and Isaac (Gen. 22:1-19), or the father waiting for his prodigal son to return home (Lk. 15). The father immediately embraced his wayward son. The father eagerly welcomed his son home. He didn't demean or belittle his son. He didn't wash his son's face in his mistakes or past failures. He remained a faithful loving Daddy in spite of the son's transgressions and shortcomings.

**Train up a child in the way he should go. Even when he is old he will not depart from it.
Proverbs 22:6 NLT**

This Daddy warmly embraced his repentant son. He eagerly showered his son with Daddy's hugs, Daddy's kisses, and Daddy's love. A healthy hug shouldn't be taken for granted. According to Virginia Satir, "We need four hugs for survival. We need eight hugs a day for maintenance. We need twelve hugs a day for growth." Many people go weeks, months, and even years without ever coming near this quota.

Fathers don't aggravate your children. If you do, they will become discouraged and quit trying. Colossians 3:21 NLT

Kim also had another habit. She knew how to get exactly what she wanted from her Daddy.

We would ask her, "Kim, how do you have your Daddy?"

She would wiggle her finger, "Wrapped around my finger."

Every child and parent has an emotional need that determines how the family will respond to love, fear, prejudice, hate, anger, and in time of crisis. The family must provide unconditional love, hugs, discipline, support, commitment, appreciation, acceptance, realistic and obtainable expectations, individual space, family activities, relationship building, unity, trust, and respect for each other. "I love you" must be said sincerely and frequently.

What exactly is it that you expect of me?
Please define it for me?
Is it something that I could never be?
Is it something that I don't know how to be?

My Scars

"There was a time when father amounted to something in the United States. He was held with some esteem in the community; he had some authority in his own household; his views were sometimes taken seriously by his children; and even his wife paid heed to him from time to time."—Adlai E. Stevenson

On Wednesday morning, July 11, 1962, while standing near her bedroom closet, Evelyn Russell heard a voice speak.

"What would you do if Herman died?"

The young wife threw her arms up and waved them towards heaven. "Oh Lord, don't let me even think about that."

The thought of him dying was too unbearable. She loved him so much that she wore her hair to suit his taste. If there was a dress that he liked, she wore the dress two days straight if that made him happy. His favorite dessert was banana pudding. Early in their relationship, her mother made the dessert for him. This had to change.

She thought within her, "I'm going to learn to make banana pudding for my own husband."

If she thought that she had imagined the voice, one-week later, she knew it had been the voice of God. The next Wednesday morning, her mother rushed to her bedroom with a telegram. Ma'Dear remained at the door, as her daughter read the telegram.

"Oh Ma'Dear, Herman is dead!"

"No he's not Evelyn. You must be reading it wrong."

Ma'Dear took the telegram from her daughter's hand. After she finished reading it, they both burst into tears.

On Wednesday July 18, 1962, shortly after the dawning of a new day, a decision was made that would dramatically affect a number of lives for years. A young solider decided that another soldier would never enjoy the beauty of that day. As Herman Russell Jr. sat in his car waiting for a train to clear the railroad tracks, he was brutally murdered. On this warm summer night in Hopkinsville, Kentucky, the soldier sat in his car with the windows rolled down. Another soldier approached the car and proceeded to take the life that he didn't give. He stabbed the twenty-five-year-old soldier numerous times. The perpetrator of the crime was another twenty-two year old soldier. It was reported that the young soldiers were involved in an earlier altercation. The circumstances surrounding the incident remain cloudy to me. The aftermath of this incident is very clear.

Herman Russell, Jr. left a twenty-two-year-old widow and a three-year-old child to morn his passing. Soon another child would join the mourning. The young widow was two months pregnant with the couple's second child, Crystal. This death would leave a resounding effect on the children who would never know Daddy's hugs, Daddy's kisses, and Daddy's love.

As Mama sat holding me on her lap at the funeral, she felt a shield of protection covering her. She knew that God was protecting her and the unborn child that she was carrying, the child that her husband would never see. My grandfather had warned my mother.

"If you look at a dead person, your baby will be born blind."

Mama didn't tell him, but inwardly, she had her own thoughts.

"I don't believe that God would let my baby be born blind because I looked at her Daddy."

The LORD hears His people when they call to Him for help. He rescues them from all their troubles. The LORD is close to the brokenhearted;
He rescues those who are crushed in spirit.
The righteous face many troubles, but the LORD rescues them from each and every one. For the LORD protects them from harm—not one of their bones will be broken!
Psalm 34:17-20 NLT

On Monday, January 28, 1963, at approximately 1:30 A.M. Crystal Hermine Russell made her screaming entrance into the world. She was born at Martin Army Hospital in Fort Benning, GA. She was a child who would never see her father; as such, she was supposed to have special healing powers.

The old folks said, "If a baby has thrash, all you need to cure it is get someone who has never seen their father to blow in their mouth."

Something must have been wrong with Crystal's healing powers. They had her blow into the mouths of many babies. She blew into many of the children's mouths in the project when they had thrash. I never saw one of them cured. That didn't stop them from trying.

In my deepest times of loneliness, I imagined what my life would be like if I had been given the opportunity to know my father. My images of him were the only symbols of perfection in my life. I felt cheated, deprived, and robbed of all semblance of normalcy by this person, who had murdered my Daddy, when I was three years old. I often wondered if this murderer knew what he had done to my life, if he had any understanding of the depth of the pain that he had forced into my life. I couldn't understand how my mother could forgive the person who had single-handedly wrecked my life. Shortly after murdering my father, the murderer wrote my mother a letter apologizing for murdering him. Mama quickly decided to accept his plea for forgiveness.

I never received a courtesy letter, requesting my forgiveness. Over the years, I asked myself, "Did the murderer know about me? Did he think about me? Did he think about how this incident would affect me? Did he care about me? Was he concerned about my pain?" The answers always came back, "No." No, he never gave more than a fleeting thought to how this death would affect a three-year-old child. It never occurred to anyone that years later this incident would haunt this three-year-old child. After all, how do you explain death to a three-year-old?

When the murderer waved his murderous dagger, repeatedly striking my father, his anger gave no place for reason. There were no thoughts of how this act of violence would affect his life or the lives of others. There was anger raging inside of him that was looking for a vent. This anger found the ventilation that was needed. However, it marred the lives of others. It marred my life, forever.

Being a teenager can be an extremely painful period, particularly during early adolescence. It was during this period that the absence of my father began to weigh heaviest on my mind. At this time, I only knew a few of the details of my father's death. I began to grieve for a person who had been deceased for more than ten years. It was as if my father died for the second time.

How do you tell someone that you have just begun the grieving process for someone who died before you even understood the meaning of life or death? What is a teenager's understanding of grief? Who do you tell about the pain causing a war in your mind? Who will understand that you aren't losing your mind?

I developed my own image of my father. I imagined my father as perfect and faultless. You know one of those like Fred McMurray on "My Three Sons." Perhaps, Bill Cosby on "The Cosby Show" would replace Fred McMurray, if I were grieving today.

I had only two memories of ever seeing him. The first one was of him coming up the stairs at Ma'Dear's house, while my baby-sitter was giving me a bath in the bathroom at the top of the stairs. On another occasion, I was outside near the end of the apartment building when he came home on leave from the Army to visit us. We were still living with Ma'Dear then. Both times, we were thrilled to see each other.

In my deepest times of loneliness, I imagined what my life would be like if I had been given the opportunity to know my father. My images of him were the only perfect thing in my life. I would often sit alone in my misery, in the dark, playing sad songs, and thinking about my father. I sat in a dark room listening to the sadness of the Blues, having a private pity party. The songs understood my pain.

One of my favorite songs was by Carla Thomas, *What Do the Lonely Do at Christmas Time*. The lyrics went something like this, "'Tis the season to be jolly, but how can I be when I have nobody?" Another song that I listened to by Tommy James and his band went something like this, "Life cut like a knife. I'm so deeply wounded." I was left alone and isolated with my pain. Each day, I continued my masquerade of pretending everything was fine, yet inside I was dying. I was taking accelerated steps towards my private hell.

The mirror over my dresser in my bedroom served as the place where I often saw my father's handsome face peering down on me. I could look at the mirror while lying in bed. Whenever I was hurting the most, in my imagination, he was always there providing the support and encouragement that I desperately needed. The thoughts plaguing my mind were always the same.

"My life would be so different if you had lived."

How did his death affect Crystal? She was always easily excitable. Mama said it was because she cried so much when she was pregnant with her. Mama gave her special attention because of this. Later, Crystal had crying children.

One day, Crystal saw on the news that prisoners of war were being released. She knew in her heart that our father was dead, but she watched television all day waiting to hear his name. It never came. When she was about four years old, we went riding down the street. As we passed a group of soldiers standing near the edge of the street, Crystal stuck her head out window.

"Hey soldiers!"

Perhaps, she hoped that in this group, she would find the face of her father. I don't know. I never thought about it until today. Maybe the fascination wasn't with them, but her father. Could this have been a cry for Daddy's hugs, Daddy's kisses, and Daddy's love…?

Once, when Crystal was sick, she had a comforting visit. Maybe it was just her imagination. She looked at the light in the corner of our room. There it was that she saw the face of her concerned father.

But I lavish my love on those who love me and obey my commands, even for a thousand generations. Exodus 20:6

The strained relationship with our father's parents only contributed to the confusion in our lives. There was no tangible foundation to build a bridge to knowing our father. If his family had been a more active part of our lives, perhaps we would have known my father through their memories. This was just another part of my confusion. However, I don't think that anyone could have been an adequate substitute, in his absence.

There were many people who tried to compensate. Uncle Ruben developed a special love for Crystal. He gave her an allowance each week, bought her presents, and helped with high school expenses.

Over the years, things that belonged to Daddy were held dear. We each had a period where we wore his bomber jacket to school. Mama kept the dress that she wore when they were married. She also kept the dress that I wore to his funeral. She still has both dresses. They are worn and discolored from the passing of time. Her memory of him is still extremely vivid and colorful. She will never willingly depart from the two dresses.

My mother had kept every letter that my father had ever written her during his tour of duty. She had duffel bags full of these letters in her bedroom closet. At the time of his murder, my father was Airborne and had been stationed in Fort Campbell, Kentucky. He had written my mother regularly during the times that they were separated. I decided that I would read each and every letter that he had sent her.

I was searching for answers, searching to know him. The times that my mother was working provided the perfect opportunity for me to carry out my mission. I was determined to find my answers, regardless of the cost. For hours each day, I read these letters. I read until I was positive that I had read each of them thoroughly. The letters only enhanced my views of my perfect and faultless father. They also served to push me further from my mother.

In some of my loneliest hours and moments of reflections, I wrote poems that expressed my feelings. The things that I couldn't express audibly, the pains that I couldn't share with anyone were written down. During this time, I wrote poems on a daily basis. They expressed the pain in my heart. This was the only outlet for the pain. The pain has gotten better over the years. The depression took flight long ago. Nevertheless, the scars remain.

For years, I didn't understand how something seemingly so natural and simple could scar someone's entire life. It was only while writing a paper in graduate school that I discovered how deeply my father's death had influenced my life. The strange thing about this was that the assignment should have been simple and totally unrelated.

Over the years, I have taken a number of counseling courses and written more papers than I care to remember. The class was vocational and career counseling. We were to write a twenty-page paper on how we arrived at our current career choice. The instructions were to start from the time that we were children and to conclude with our present career choice.

It was while exploring my career choices that I realized how my father's death had affected most of the decisions in my life. It was extremely painful for me to complete this assignment. In tears, I completed a simple assignment that helped to identify the root of the dysfunctions in my life. This was another step on my road to recovery and healing. I was recovering from the lack of Daddy's hugs, Daddy's kisses, and Daddy's love...

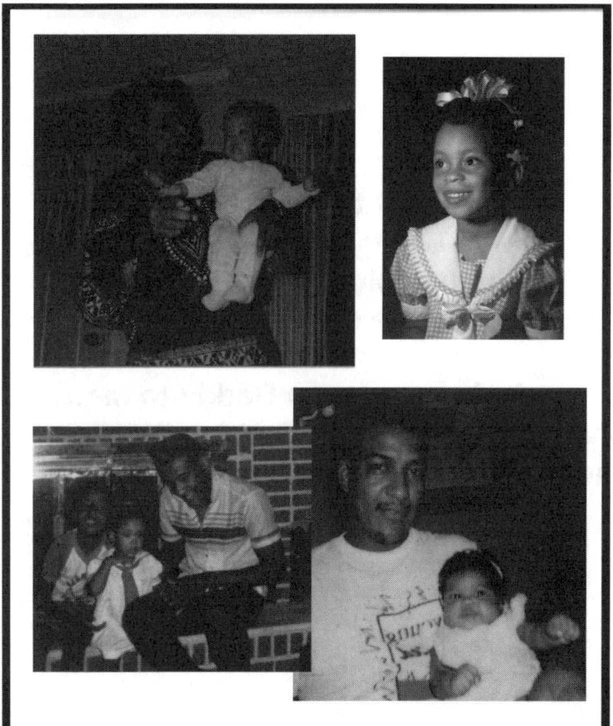

**A daughter to my mother?
Is that what you expect me to be?
That's a bit confusing to me....
She's trying to be something she could never be...
A Mommy and a Daddy to me...
So what is it that you expect me to rise above?
I had no Daddy's hugs, no Daddy's kisses, and no Daddy's love...**

A Daughter to my Mother?

Honour thy father and mother; which is the first commandment with promise;
Ephesians 6:2

When I was a young child, I was already very serious minded. I wasn't athletically inclined or overly concerned about children's games. Most of my time was spent watching soap operas or reading books. My homework was usually completed before the teacher assigned it. If I completed assignments that were never required, I didn't care. I didn't like the pressure of completing tasks on short notice. Usually, before the teacher explained an assignment, I had already figured out a short cut. I had my way of doing everything. This made it difficult to learn the teacher's method. The teachers didn't seem to object; the answers were correct.

Crystal's birthday and my birthday are five days apart. Therefore, Mama always made us celebrate our birthdays together. I hated the parties that were not quite celebrations. Mama cooked barbecue ribs, chicken, chitterlings, hot dogs with homemade chili, potato salad, collard greens, black-eyed peas, macaroni and cheese, candied yams, homemade ice cream, and a variety of cupcakes. Once we even had a three-tier wedding cake.

Why did I hate the parties? Mama said that anybody could come to our parties. There were no boundaries. They didn't have to be our friends. Even if they hated us, they could come to the parties. It seemed there were always more adults present than there were children. Mama had one stipulation; no one could bring us a gift.

"I wanted everyone to be free to come. I didn't want a present to keep them from coming."

She said that we had everything. There was one thing that we didn't have, Daddy. We didn't have Daddy's hugs, Daddy's kisses, and Daddy's love.

By the time I was in the fifth grade, I was already learning to cook. In the sixth grade, we had a party at school. I made a cake that was shaped and decorated like a castle. Ice cream cones were used for the towers of the castle, and I used pieces of a Hershey's candy bar for the windows and doors. We barbecued almost every Sunday and I assisted Mama with this task. In the sixth grade, I also cooked my first complete meal, meatloaf, baked potatoes, string beans, and rolls. For dessert, I made a pear salad. It was decorated to resemble a rabbit. A pear half was placed on a leaf of lettuce. Marshmallows and maraschino cherries were used to decorate the pear. I had gotten the recipes from a cookbook at the library.

In the seventh grade, I learned to sew in Home Economics class. Mama bought me a sewing machine that Christmas. Crystal had long legs and it was hard to find pants that were long enough for her legs. I began making her clothes. I never made her dresses. She hated dresses. Mama had given her a dress, once. Crystal took it in the bedroom and tried to burn it. She was a real tomboy. On the other hand, I had issues that were more adult, on my mind. By the time I was in the eighth grade, other people were paying me to sew for them.

On Saturdays, we usually cleaned the house thoroughly. Mama loved Barry White and his music was usually playing as we cleaned the house. Mama and Crystal would dance in the hall and in front of the mirror. I usually watched and laughed. I didn't have the coordination. Crystal was the real dancer in the family.

Girls are trained to be wives and mothers, learning primarily from the example of their own mothers. The mother trains up her daughters with the skills to run the household, and prepares them for their eventual role as wife and mother. However, not all is so happy in families where husbands are deceased, or where husbands are abusive. The father's relationship with his daughter will guide her views of other men.

Somewhere and somehow, things changed.

Mama said, "One day, I woke up with a stranger in the house."

It may have seemed that way to her but the storm had been brewing for years. There was something missing within me. When I began acting out and rebelling, Mama tried to discipline me. This only made me rebel more. I began running away, usually to Ma'Dear's house. There were no demands there. Ma'Dear was easygoing and very protective. I began to cleave to her. This was something that I would reap years later.

Many people have asked me, "Who bought you those hot clothes you wore as a teenager." Mama bought me lots of THINGS to try to make me happy. Usually, when she disciplined me, later that day, she was sorry. A shopping trip was sure to follow. This eventually got old. I resented her trying to appease me. I knew when I was getting away with too much. It seemed the only times that I got in real trouble was when I was innocent.

On the corner of one of the apartment rows in Warren Williams, there was a tree. From one of the windows in our apartments, I could hear a crowd of young men at night. Each night, they gathered under the tree to gamble. The only light illuminating the spot was the streetlight on a nearby pole. I couldn't tell what they were doing, only that they seemed to be having lots of fun. Early one morning, I decided to check out the tree. There were pennies, nickels, dimes, and quarters left under the tree. From that moment on, every morning, I got up early and slipped out of the house. I went to check "The Money Tree." When Mama noticed all the money that I was collecting, she questioned me. She didn't believe that I had found a Money Tree. She punished me but I had told the truth. This stopped my morning trips.

Many people wrongly assume that the mother alone provides for the molding and shaping of the daughter's personality and character. However, it's from her father that the daughter gains her inner identity. She learns to relate to other men by watching how her father treats her mother. This is where she learns what to expect from a relationship with a male. If the father treats the mother with disrespect, the daughter learns to accept this treatment from men. On the other hand, if the father treats the mother with love and respect, his daughter learns to expect this treatment from men. This was a missing link in my life.

Pam relates this story.
"When I was young I thought that I had the best Daddy in the world. He was a good provider, but he never told me anything. He didn't discipline me. He never corrected me. He went to work and came home. He would sit in his chair and chew on his cigar. It was almost as if he was a robot. We even put pins in his chair to see if that would make him move. That didn't even work. Mama would give him a grocery list and he would bring home everything on it. He was so predictable. We could copy Mama's handwriting. We would add things to the list like ice cream cones and candy. When he brought the bags home, we would rush to get everything out the bag before Mama saw it. We got away with that for almost five years. I thought he was the best Daddy in the world, until I started dating. My father didn't prepare me for the world. When I started dating, I was looking for a man like my Daddy. I wanted a man who would sit down and shut-up. Needless to say, I never found one like that."

I once heard a story. Whether it's true or not, I cannot say. The father came home and beat the mother. The mother beat the children. The children in return beat the cat. Each person passed on the treatment that was received to someone else.

The Father's role is as important as that of the mother. They each have very distinct but equally important roles. You don't have to review research to verify this important fact. Ask the mother of any successful family and if there are doubts still lingering, ask the single mother who is struggling to fulfill the role of both father and mother.

My mother tried to compensate for the absence of my father. How could she fill the void left by his absence? There was a place in my heart reserved especially for Daddy. There was no replacement or substitute worthy to fulfill his place. There was no way a mother, uncle, or stepfather could ever fill the void left by Daddy's absence. Any efforts by anyone else to fill that role only brought additional confusion and resentment. Their roles became cloudy and confusing. Is there a suitable replacement for any Daddy?

We can empathize or sympathize with a person that is experiencing a loss, but we can never fill the void. I resented Mama for trying to compensate. I loved her, but I was confused about the pain in my heart. It seemed that out of nowhere the grief set in, and I couldn't shake it. It wasn't something that I wanted to feel. There were days when everything was going fine and I didn't think about him as much. However, on the days when things went wrong, I longed for his presence.

The Bible clearly indicates that the husband and father in a family is to be the spiritual head of that family. This is a high calling and the holy duty of Christian men. This does not suggest that in so doing that faithful Christian women who must step into the role of the spiritual head are doing something wrong, or that their family is spiritually lost.

This is not meant to imply that women without a husband and without a father in their family are incapable of providing spiritual leadership for their family. Nor is it meant to imply that the role of the husband and father is somehow not a part of God's intention for families. We live in a time when sadly, many men view matters of the faith as "for women" and take a less active role in their families' spiritual growth than God expects them to take. He expects them to actively lead the family.

God's ways are as hard to discern as the pathways of the wind, and as mysterious as a tiny baby being formed in a mother's womb. Ecclesiastes 11:5 NLT

When I became pregnant with my first child at the age of fourteen, I had all the answers. I knew everything my mother did wrong. She had done a few things right. However, there were so many more that she had done wrong. There was no way I was going to make any of her mistakes. I had all the right answers. My child would have the perfect mother and perfect home. Daddy wasn't in my plan. Why did the child need a Daddy? You know they say that you can't miss something that you never had. Is this statement really true? Is possible that I didn't have all the answers? Is there a place within each child reserved just for Daddy? Can you miss Daddy's hugs, Daddy's kisses, and Daddy's love…?

A mother to my child…
Why would you expect that of me?
I've got my own issues, can't you see?
There is still a hole inside of me….
No one has defined a man's love for me…
I had no Daddy's hugs, no Daddy's kisses, and no Daddy's love…

A Mother to my Child?

Behold, Children are a gift of the Lord; the fruit of the womb is a reward. Like arrows in the hand of a warrior, so are the children of one's youth. How blessed is the man whose quiver is full of them...Psalm 127:3-5

On October 2, 1974, at the age of 15, at about 1:30 P.M., my **first** pregnancy resulted in the birth of an 8lb 5oz baby girl. She looked just like Ma'Dear. The long thick straight hair on her head reminded me of Ma'Dear's wig. I named the child after her. Ma'Dear's real name was Earline Emmaline Nettie Pearl Odessa Owens Alexander. I didn't do the child that bad; I took the Earline and left off the rest. I gave her Mama's middle name, Lavern.

Earline was and still is the most beautiful baby that I had ever seen. My baby was born less than an hour after I arrived at Martin Army Hospital. It was definitely the child of my youth.

That morning while sitting at the breakfast table eating a breakfast that consisted of smoked sausage, scrambled eggs with cheese, cheese grits, hot chocolate, and a pomegranate for dessert, I began to have indigestion. At least, I thought it was indigestion. It wasn't bad, but it was annoying. This wasn't the first time that this happened during my pregnancy. I attributed it to my healthy appetite. The pomegranate would later be a point of contention.

During my pregnancy, I was careful not to take any medications that were not approved by a doctor. I kept the books that the clinic had given me handy. Before doing anything, that I wasn't sure of, I checked the baby books. All of the antacids were ruled out as possibilities. I called Ma'Dear for one of the home remedies. She usually had one and if not she knew who to call. Ma'Dear told me that eating a spoon of mustard was good for curing indigestion. I ate a big spoon of mustard, but the mustard didn't relieve my symptoms.

It was always difficult to reach the medical staff at Martin Army Hospital by telephone. This day was no exception. I tried calling several times. After being unable to reach the hospital by telephone, Ma'Dear called Mama at work to tell her what was happening. Mama decided that it was best to drive me to Martin Army. My bag was already in the car. We had been to the hospital several times with false labor pains.

When we arrived on the labor and delivery ward of the hospital, the nurse informed me that my baby would be born within the hour. This scared Mama and me. I don't know which of us was more afraid. Mama was concerned about her child. I was concerned that the pain was going to get worse. The screams and curses of the other women in the labor area escalated my fears. I was shaking so badly from fear that I couldn't push during the contractions. I had heard too many horror stories about childbirth.

The day that I had feared since I found out Martin Army believed in natural childbirth was at hand. Early in my pregnancy, I had been pressured to abort my baby, and I had adamantly refused. During my first prenatal examination at Martin Army, they told me that I would have natural childbirth unless it became necessary for me to have a Cesarean birth. This made me consider the abortion, momentarily. That was until they told me that they wouldn't put me to sleep to have the abortion either. Now in the labor and delivery ward, scared already by the unknown and all the horror stories that I had heard about childbirth, the women screaming in the ward made me change my mind about having a baby. It was too late to change the course of nature. My body was committed whether I liked it or not. I was scared that soon I would be hurting like these women. My legs and hands were trembling so much that I couldn't help with the delivery process. The nurses had to hold my legs for me. Mama was constantly beating my hands trying to reassure me.

"It's going to be all right baby."

She was hurting my hand more than the labor pains were hurting. I wanted to reassure her so that she would stop beating me.

My baby was born within the hour, exactly as the nurse had estimated. The pains never got any worse than the pains of indigestion. There was no father present in the labor room. It never occurred to me that he needed to be there. All I had was a desire to call him and let him know when the baby was born. I wasn't expecting anything from him. Nothing in my world indicated that I should expect anything from him. My world consisted of women raising their children alone. I knew of some cases where fathers were present, but that didn't impress me.

After the child's birth, I was so weak that I was barely able to make it to the nursery to see her. She was born so fast that she caused a complication, which forced me to remain on a liquid diet, for the remainder of my stay in the hospital.

In the delivery room, the nurse said, "Stop pushing."

I responded, "I'm not."

The delivery was over that fast. Thus, I was on a diet consisting of broth, Jell-O, and bananas for three days. The whole time I was thinking, 'when I get home, and this is over; I am going to eat my pomegranate.' Wouldn't you know it; Crystal had already eaten it. To make matters worse, it was the end of the season for the fruit. It would be almost a year before I could get another one.

There was one amazing thing about returning home. My bed was full of presents for the baby. The neighbors had brought them. They were all from my favorite store. They knew we shopped at the Kiddie Shoppe.

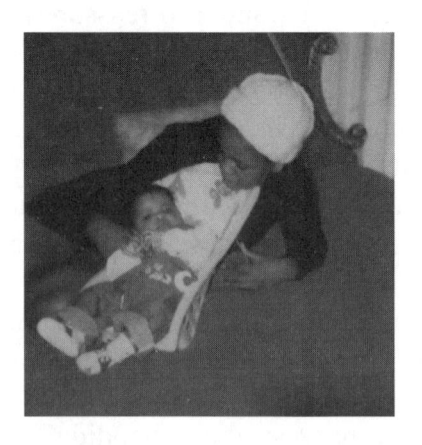

The mothers bare the children, nurse them, and raise them primarily in their early years. She holds the household together by performing a wide variety of tasks. However, this does not negate the importance of the father during this period. Proverbs 31:10-31 gives us a good description of the honor accorded the mother of the house. She was far from docile and subservient, as she had to be quite bold to fulfill her role.

Although, I was only fifteen, I understood the importance of breast-feeding the baby. I breast-fed her. When I went back to school the next month, I pumped bottles of milk to leave for her. However, school soon made it impossible to continue this tradition. She was placed on can milk.

Recently, I observed sixteen-month-old Kayla, as her father came home from work. She recognized the sound of his car before he ever entered the house. She began to scream so loud that it sounded like a crowd at a football game. It seemed impossible that one small body could make so much noise. Next, she began to run back and forth to the door. When he entered the house, her outstretched arms demanded to be picked up. As soon as she was securely in his arms, she laid her head on his shoulder. She was so quiet and content that you could hear a pin fall. Her father stated, "This is the way that she responds, each time I return home." This response was not reserved for the mother. This was bonding time that she needed with her father.

When I was sent to prison, in 1986, my most grievous task involved my children. To aid my mother to effectively-care for my children, I needed to give her temporary custody of them. Although this was temporary, this was the hardest part of being locked up. The loss of custody seemed permanent in my mind. It seemed that I was losing them forever.

I prided myself on taking good care of my children. Even during the times when I wasn't hustling and my finances were tight, I found money to take them shopping regularly. I thought spending money on them made me a good parent. They spent a lot of time with Mama because I didn't want them exposed to the streets, but I was always able to pick them up. The day that my lawyer brought the papers to the jail for me to sign was one of the hardest days that I spent incarcerated.

When my lawyer arrived, I was summoned outside of the cell to meet with him in a private room. When asked to sign the papers, I became upset. As I cried, he assured me that all Mama had to do was give me my children back when I returned home. Still, I was giving up my parental rights. "Temporally" didn't make this easier. I didn't understand that the paper didn't make me a good mother. Custody didn't make me a good mother. Buying gifts didn't make me a mother. Being a good parent is more than a formality.

When I returned home from prison, I reaped something that I had sown. My relationship with my son, Herman, hadn't changed. However, my relationship with Earline had been severely altered. She was having her own crisis. Not only had she missed her mother, she missed her father. She blamed me for her holes, for the unhappiness. She was moody and cranky. I wanted to help her but it seemed that she resented me. She didn't talk to me about her feelings. Instead, she began to cleave to Mama, the same way that I had cleaved to Ma'Dear.

As a teenager, Earline developed a slogan, "Who needs a father when you've got a mother?"

I assumed this was because of some of the things that I did, not because there was a hole in her life. When things break around the house, my first response is always to attempt to repair them. When the car breaks down, my response is the same. Over the years, I put in an alternator, a water pump, took the carburetor off to be rebuilt and replaced it, changed fan belts, assisted with oil changes, and replaced electrical parts. At one point, I had a full tool chest. When I got my first new car, Mr. Charlie asked me to put my tool kit up. I no longer do car repairs. Nevertheless, should an emergency arise, I have no intentions of waiting patiently by the side of the road for help.

About three years ago, the car broke down as my children were driving home from college. Herman was driving at some accelerated speed, as Earline slept. When Earline woke up, the car was slowing until it finally stopped along the interstate. Herman informed his sister that he had almost won a race against another vehicle. We are not sure how fast the car was traveling. The speedometer flipped over at 100 m.p.h.

It was a Sunday afternoon when they called me. They were near Newnan, Georgia, south of Atlanta and about 60 miles from Columbus. For some reason, the circuit to our roadside service was busy. I continued calling, but I was on my way to bring them and the car home. By the time I reached them, I was still unsuccessful in reaching the roadside service. After being unable to repair the car on the spot, I gave Earline her instructions.

"Place the car in neutral, turn on the emergency flashers; I'm going to push the car to Columbus. It's getting dark and we're not going to be stuck here at night."

Herman knew that he was at fault. The car overheated and he chose to ignore it. That coupled with his love for Earline made him climb in the back seat of the car. He didn't want her to ride alone. It never occurred to me that we wouldn't make it home. I pushed the car down the interstate. With Mama and La'Toya in my new Maxima, I pulled up behind her. I pushed the car to the shop in Columbus. There was only one glitch. As we turned from Airport Thruway on to Veteran's Parkway, a policeman was stopped at the adjacent red light. Earline managed to hide the push by turning into a vacant parking lot. After the officer passed, we completed the trip. In about an hour, we made it home safely. However, I had to buy a new tag for the front of my car. Warning, please don't try this stunt. This was just one of those times that I responded out of necessity. Earline had one thought all the way to Columbus.

"I'm going to die in front of my child."

Thus, I ask the following questions. This is not to imply that my mother was a bad mother or to excuse my own stupidity. How was I supposed to know what a good mother was supposed to be? Who showed me what a family was meant to be? Who told me what a good mother was supposed to be? Who showed me what was expected of me? How was I supposed to know that good mothers give careful thought to who they choose to father their children? Who defined my femininity? Who told me what my children needed from me? There were too many holes inside of me. There were pains that no one could see. I had never developed a healthy identity. I didn't understand what motherhood was meant to be. I had no special friend, no special Daddy. I had no Daddy's hugs, no Daddy's kisses, and no Daddy's love…

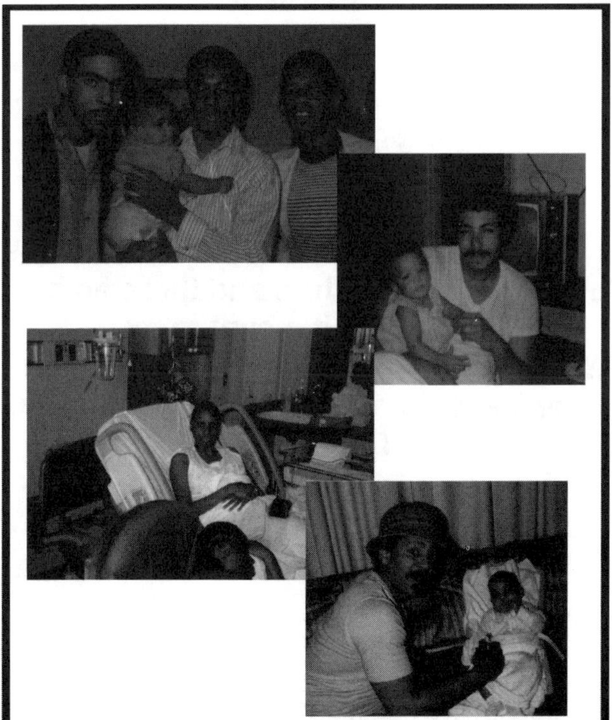

A father to my daughter…
Did you really expect that of me?
Coddle her, hold her, reassure her…
Is that what you really expected from me?
Fondle her, molest her, and threaten her….
That's what it meant to me…
Who was my example supposed to be?
I had no Daddy's hugs, no Daddy's kisses, and no Daddy's love…

A Father to my Daughter?

Kim went to visit Aunt Bobbie one summer. Aunt Bobbie said Kim talked about her Daddy all night. When she finished talking about him, she burst into tears. Her Daddy went to Atlanta one weekend. He stopped by to see Kim and told her he was planning to go to Six Flags the next day. She wanted to go with him. The next day, he picked Kim up for the trip to the Adventure Park. When the day was over, she didn't want to be separated from her father. She didn't want to return to Aunt Bobbie's house to pick up her belongings. She only wanted to be with her Daddy.

Buck has a very special relationship with our granddaughter, La'Toya. She has him, as the expression goes "wrapped around her fingers." Whatever La'Toya wants, La'Toya gets, no matter what else goes lacking. She calls him "Grand Daddy Buck." Several years ago, she requested that he purchase her a Barbie bicycle for Christmas. Different people had already purchased two bicycles for that Christmas. Nevertheless, they weren't Barbie bicycles and that was what La'Toya had asked for. He promised La'Toya that she would get the bicycle that she wanted for Christmas. I explained to him that she would receive two bicycles for Christmas, as gifts.

That didn't matter to him; she wanted a Barbie bicycle. I explained to him that I needed the money for something else. I even suggested buying Barbie stickers to put on one of the other bikes. In the end, La'Toya won. There was never any doubt that she would.

During one our numerous separations, he called me. He wanted me to take him to a store to get La'Toya the biggest Easter basket that he could find. I agreed, knowing he had made her another promise. When we got to the store, he picked the biggest basket. However, he was dissatisfied with it. It didn't have everything that she wanted in it. There was no basket anywhere with everything, which he had promised to her. Therefore, he bought videotapes, additional bags of candy, and toys to put in the basket. He wasn't concerned about the cost. It was what his baby wanted. Afterwards, I asked him to buy some gas for my car. This was just a test.

He casually responded, "I don't have any more money."

It is understood that La'Toya's favorite person is "Grand Daddy Buck." He developed this bond with La'Toya when she was a baby. La'Toya stayed with us while Earline was away in college. When La'Toya was a baby, he gave her lots of Grand Daddy's hugs, Grand Daddy's kisses, and Grand Daddy's love…

When Earline was a baby, Ma'Dear would bathe her in the kitchen sink. As she began to talk, Earline had one stipulation. No males were allowed in the house when she took her bath. If she heard what she perceived to be a male voice, she screamed as loud as she could.

"Don't come in this house."

I don't know where she developed this phobia. However, it may not have been such a bad idea.

Do not have sexual intercourse with your sister or half sister, whether she is your father's daughter or your mother's daughter, whether she was brought up in the same family or somewhere else. Leviticus 18:9 NLT

Several years ago, I was facilitating a group of approximately twenty-five teenage girls. The group began discussing rape. In the course of the discussion, most of the girls revealed that someone who was trusted by their family had inappropriately touched them. The perpetrators were fathers, stepfathers, grandfathers, brothers, uncles, siblings' boyfriends, and the list went on. Where did these men learn this inappropriate behavior? On the other hand, more appropriately, where was it that they failed to learn the appropriate behavior? Who was their example? Who was supposed to teach them how to treat a young woman? Who was entrusted with the responsibility of training them to be real men?

In the New Testament, Jesus refers to God as Abba, our equivalent to Daddy, Father, or Papa. This is an obvious term for a close and loving relationship. The paternal relationship was never meant to cause physical, emotional, social, or spiritual pain. God established the husband/father position as the provider for the family. The most important gift that the father provides to his children is love. Timothy teaches that a neglectful father was worse than a pagan was.

But if any provide not for his own, and especially for those of his own house, he hath denied the faith, and is worse than an infidel.
I Tim. 5:8

When I was teenage girl, vegetable-trucks brought fresh vegetables and fruit to the projects. Usually, the truck stopped near the front door of our apartment. Whenever the old man from across the ditch saw me at truck, he was quick to buy me whatever I wanted from the vegetable man. Then he would invite me to come over to his house. I took the fruit, but the look in his eyes warned me not to go that way. Ironically, his wife had taken us to church for years. Her husband never went to church. This is just one example of the numerous times that men looked at me and I felt like a piece of meat.

At eight months old, Kayla was unable to tell her father from one of her uncles, as she looked at rear view of him. She couldn't tell their voices apart. His brother decided to trick her, in an attempt to hold her. As her uncle slowly turned, Kayla ran screaming, "Dada, Dada, Dada."

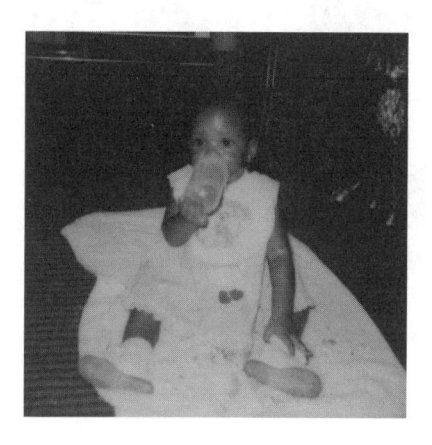

My niece, Ashley was a real crybaby. Ma'Dear said that Crystal had screaming babies. It was extremely difficult to keep Ashley. My husband, Buck started rubbing her ears to keep her quiet. He rubbed her ears until she would fall off to sleep. As she grew older, he fed her Cheetos, as he rubbed her ears. When she grew older, Ashley developed a bad habit. She liked to rub ears, anybody's ears. This included the new babies' ears. Her grandmother said that she could kill Buck for starting this habit. Today, Ashley is fourteen. She still rubs ears, Daddy's ears.

When Brandon was in elementary school, Tyron dressed him for school each day. He creased Brandon's clothes to perfection. After he was dressed, Tyron dabbed his cologne behind Brandon's ears. Brandon's teachers commented about how good Brandon smelled each day. The teachers developed a fondness for the cologne and its owner, Tyron. They didn't know that he was married. The teachers told Courtney that they liked her father. They began sending messages home by the children and buying them ice cream. The children thought it was funny. One day, Tyron was requested to come to the school, Crystal went with him. The teachers ignored her.

Each of Tyron's children knows the difference between his car and Crystal's car. They can hear the sound of his car (a quiet car) before he pulls in the driveway. They line up at the door waiting for him to enter the house.

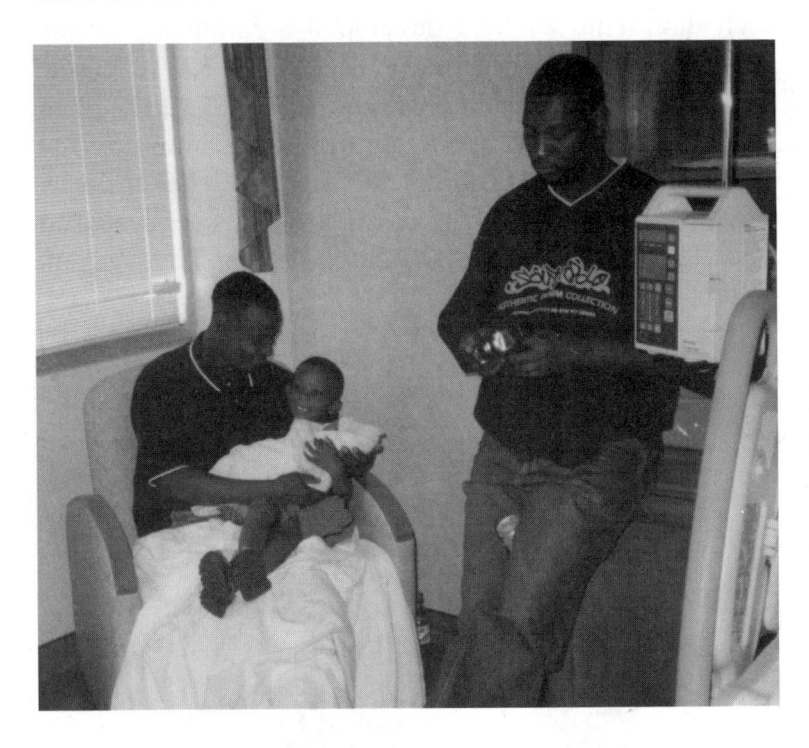

Part of what has contributed to his children's love for him is his attitude towards them. He was excited with each of the children's birth as if they were the first child. With each birth, he slept on the floor in Crystal's room. Before Crystal ever combed the girl's fine hair, Daddy had made cute ponytails on each of their heads.

The commandment to honor parents is noted by Paul as the only commandment of the Decalogue, which bore a distinct promise. The law condemned disrespect towards parents as one of the worst crimes. My mother often told us, "A disobedient child lives half his days." It is to the recognized theory of parental authority and supremacy that the various uses of the term "father" in Scripture are attributed. Whether a father walks in the role of Daddy or not will ultimately affect his descendants.

When Crystal was in labor with Kayla, the other children had an argument. Actually, it was about ten minutes before Kayla made her grand entrance into the world. The other children were at home waiting. Tyron and I were in the room with Crystal. My cell phone rang. It was one of the four children at home. They were in the midst of an argument. Their voices were so loud that cell phone served as a microphone. I gave Tyron the cell phone to resolve the crisis. There was one problem. Their voices all sounded alike with the screaming.

Not to be deterred, Tyron said, "Which one is this?"

After he finished with the first child, he said, "Put the next one on the phone."

When he finished with the third child, he had one final instruction. "Act Cameron's age because acting your age is not working."

Cameron is the only one who wasn't screaming. Cameron was four years old at the time. Within seconds of finishing with the children at home, Kayla was born. The doctor insisted that I cut half of the umbilical cord, and Tyron cut the other half.

Courtney was born at Martin Army, and due to their strict rules, I wasn't able to be in the delivery room when she was born. I missed Brandon's birth because I was in prison. With Ashley, I missed it because I was shopping with Buck. Crystal decided to put a permanent relaxer in Mama's hair before she went to the hospital. I just didn't believe that she was in labor. With Cameron and Kayla, I was present. With the last child, Nicholas, I was in the waiting room.

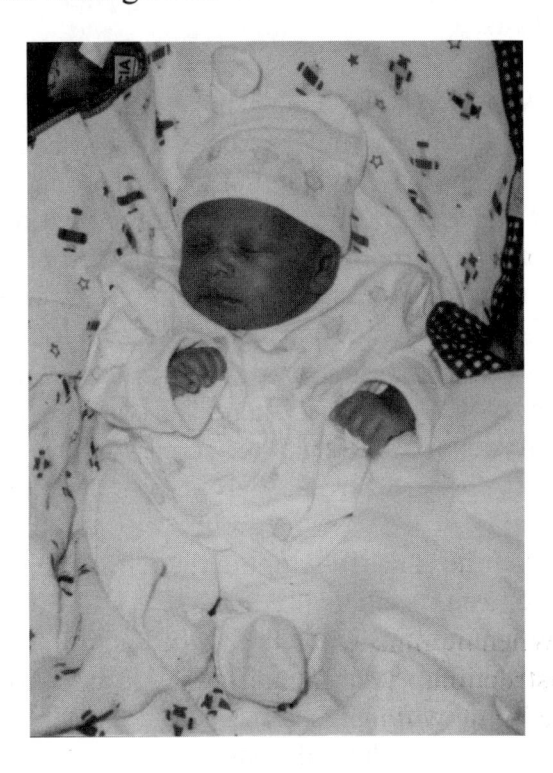

What happens when the father is totally absent from the child's life? My daughter's father was basically absent from her life. Skin, her father only came back home a couple of times over the years. The times that he was in town were the only times that he did anything for my baby. When Earline was born, I had no expectations from her father. What was I supposed to expect from him? Marriage was out of the question. I was just a young girl that he had a physical relationship with when it suited his needs. My needs were never a concern in the relationship. During the pregnancy, this didn't change. When my daughter was born, it didn't change. She was my daughter, and that was all that mattered to me. Whenever I thought of her, it was as "my daughter." I never thought of her as our daughter or referred to her in that way. I assured him that my daughter needed nothing from him. Based on my experiences, this was the truth.

Skin had been in Germany for several months when Earline was born. He remained in Germany after her birth. Earline was almost two years old when he saw her, for the first time. We wrote sporadically during his absence, and sometimes I even called him. However, there was nothing that remotely resembled a relationship. This was more of a diversion, whenever I was lonely. Other than keeping his promise to see her when he came home, I expected nothing from him. I was quick to let him know what my expectations were of him, nothing. We didn't need him or anything that he had to offer. Earline was my responsibility. I felt completely equipped for the task.

When Skin returned to the states, he kept his promise to visit. He took my baby shopping and bought her an expensive dress, and a pair of gold earrings. He asked me if she needed anything else. This was a good gesture, but he acted as if he had done something spectacular.

It's too late to speculate on what his answer would have been, if I had responded, "She needs a Daddy." Actually, I didn't know that she needed one. I told him that I had been doing a fine job of taking care of my baby, for almost two years, by myself. She didn't need his charity or lukewarm love. This was one of the four shopping trips that he took Earline on, during his four trips home.

Over the years, Skin never showed more than a passing interest in the child. The last time he saw her, he made promises to her that he never kept, and promises that she never forgot. Despite the neglect of her father, Earline was an exceptional student, and daughter. She was the kind of child that any parent would be proud to claim.

At an early age, Earline developed a love for Ma'Dear, looking at the news, and peeping out the window to keep up with what was going on in the project. She and Ma'Dear spent hours peeping out the window. Perhaps it wasn't peeping, since they pulled the curtains back to get a good view. Earline also developed an intense love for reading. She read everything, including cereal boxes, encyclopedias, and dictionaries.

My aunt would get upset when she saw the four-year-old reading the encyclopedia.

"Ma'Dear make that girl put that encyclopedia down."

No one else read the encyclopedias. Ma'Dear let Earline do what ever she wanted to do. If anybody said anything to Earline, Ma'Dear took Earline and left the house.

When Crystal was in college, Earline decided that she would read Crystal's textbooks. As she was reading one of Crystal's Psychology books, she was discovered.

"Put my book down. You can't read it."

Earline proceeded to read the passage for her.

"Well you don't know what it means. I don't know what it means."

She then explained the meaning.

"Mama make this girl leave my books alone."

Crystal and Earline are eleven years apart. This was a hard relationship for an aunt. They argued more like sisters. Crystal and Mama had a disagreement, once. Mama threatened to put Crystal out of the house. Crystal fell at Mama's feet screaming and crying. Earline had some advice for her.

"Crystal all birds have to fly some time."

"Shut up Earline! This is my Mama."

One day, I was in the shopping center at Warren's Kiddie Shoppe with Earline. We were in the shoe department when Earline decided to share something with me.

She announced very loudly, "Mama, did you know that today is a holiday?"

I didn't know, and I guess the other customers didn't know. I made the mistake of asking, as all eyes were on Earline.

"No! What type of holiday?"

"A Gay Holiday."

"Where did you hear that from?"

"Good Morning America."

Totally embarrassed, I asked, "Earline what does gay mean?"

"You know Mama, happy people."

I was relieved; she didn't know the real meaning. Everybody in the department burst into laughter.

Earline's love for reading has been a tremendous asset. She completed two undergraduate programs at the University of Georgia. Later this year, she will complete the graduate program in Social Work. She has already passed the licensure test. She was the person who brought normality to the family when our lives were in chaos. She has been a great asset to my ministry. She still has the last three items that were given to her by her father, two pairs of NIKE tennis shoes and a Mitzi doll from Chunkey Cheese.

In excusing her son's negligence, one mother said to her grandchild, "That's just the way it normally is. The mother's family always spends more time with the children than the father's family."

Is that normal or acceptable behavior? Is that the way that it's supposed to be? Is it expected that mother's should raise the children without the support of the father or the father's family?

Each year, there are millions of children that are neglected or abused. These destructive and detrimental experiences influence the impressionable child, increasing the risks for academic, behavioral, emotional, physical and social problems throughout their life.

Earline defied these odds. Yet, there are days when the wounds bleed. I was never able to be a father or Daddy to her. For years, she wanted to contact her father. Recently, I told her that I had his address. She decided it wasn't worth the effort. However, I pray that one day the wounds heal.

Am I angry with her father for not playing a more active role in her life? Am I angry with him for not providing academic, behavioral, emotional, spiritual, physical, and social support as she faced problems in her life? Were there difficult days without his support? Were there questions that I couldn't answer? Were there days when I needed help? Were there days when it seemed that she resented me for his absence? At some point, the answer to most of the questions has been yes. There were times when I resented his absence. There were difficult days as the hole developed inside the child.

As with other issues in my life, I have had to accept responsibility for my actions or the lack thereof. At the time that Earline was born, I did what I thought was best for my child. My response to the pregnancy and the birth of the child were that of a fifteen-year-old child perpetrating as an adult. During that period, my mother was extremely shy. We had very few meaningful mother/daughter conversations, during those days. If she had attempted to reason with me, I don't think that I would have listened.

It was during this period that I was trapped deepest in the grief cycle, missing Daddy. Consequently, I had no example to follow. I had no Daddy's hugs, no Daddy's kisses, and no Daddy's love... As for Skin, I have come to realize that he had some of the same problems... no Daddy's hugs, no Daddy's kisses, and no Daddy's love... As for Earline, she had no Daddy's hugs, no Daddy's kisses, and no Daddy's love...

Hugs for Daddy
Original Author Unknown
Sung to: "Ten Little Indians"

One little, two little, three little hugs,
Four little, five little, six little hugs,
Seven little, eight little, nine little hugs,
Ten little hugs for Daddy.

One big, two big, three big hugs,
Four big, five big, six big hugs,
Seven big, eight big, nine big hugs,
Ten big hugs for Daddy.

75

**A father to my son?
How could you expect that of me?
That's the laughing one....
I still wonder where "Real Men" come from....
Who was supposed to teach that to me?
I had no Daddy's hugs, no Daddy's kisses, and
no Daddy's love...**

A Father to my Son?

Hear the clatter of hooves and the rumble of wheels as the chariots rush by. Terrified fathers run madly, without a backward glance at their helpless children. Jeremiah 47:3 NLT

I have a friend who has been deeply marred by what he perceives as Daddy's abandonment and rejection. For years, the wounds have affected his life. Moreover, yes, his wounds have bled on other's lives. He has created his own fantasy world and it is there that he resides.

And you should follow my example just as I follow Christ's. 1 Corinthians 11:1 NLT

Brandon told me that he remembers a night that he really wanted to see his father. His father was at work. He stayed awake for hours, counting the time until his father returned home. Unlike my friend, his father came home.

Parents need to be what they want their children to be. Say what they want their children to say. They must do what they want their children to do. Fathers must be so upstanding in their moral behavior that they can invite their children to imitate them. This behavior should not be based on hidden pains or myths. The father has to be true and honest with himself and his own pain. If he fails to be honest, he creates a false perception that will leave his children ill prepared to face the reality of the world.

Mannasseh was one of the most corrupt and evil men mentioned in the Bible, although, his father was the godly King Hezekiah. Mannasseh has gone down in history as being the worst king to reign over Judah (2 Kgs. 21:1-16). The wicked actions of Mannasseh are both offensive and reproachable. However, it would be difficult to read of a more righteous father than King Hezekiah.

He trusted in the Lord God of Israel; so that after him was none like him among all the kings of Judah, nor any that were before him. For he clave to the Lord, and departed not from following Him, but kept His commandments, which the Lord commanded Moses. 2 Kgs. 18: 5-6

King Hezekiah prayed for God to spare his life, after being warned by the prophet of his approaching death. God miraculously granted his request and added fifteen years to King Hezekiah's life. It was during this fifteen-year period that his wicked son, Mannasseh was born. There will be other times when this godly and ungodly father/son relationship is repeated. Some corrupt fathers will have godly children. Other godly fathers will have corrupt and immoral children.

But suppose that sinful son, in turn, has a son who sees his father's wickedness but decides against that kind of life. Ezekiel 18:14

However, God has given strict instructions that a father is to train up his children. What does the Bible say about the importance and role of fathers? The Bible makes it clear that fathers are to be primarily responsible for teaching their children about God and God's expectations for their life. This is a critically important job for any father. This responsibility should not be taken lightly or irrelevantly. Fathers are to model the Heavenly Father and serve as spiritual leaders in the home.

Train up a child in the way he should go, and when he is old he will not depart from it. Proverbs 22:6

By the time my son was born, my expectations of a father had increased somewhat. Was I expecting Robert to be an example for my son? Was I expecting him to nurture, love, protect, and teach him? Was I expecting him to provide physical, emotional, social, and spiritual support? I had two expectations of him. I wanted him in the delivery room when the child was born, and I wanted financial support for the child until he was twenty-one.

But if anyone does not provide for his own, and especially for those of his household, he has denied the faith, and is worse than an unbeliever. 1 Timothy 5:8 NLT

How did I want him to treat him? He was never to discipline MY child. I didn't trust him to discipline my son. That was my job. How was I supposed to know that was the father's job? If I had known this, it would have greatly influenced my decision to have a child with him. There is no way I would ever have agreed to him being any type of example for my child. In fact, my greatest fear with Herman was that he would be influenced by Robert's behavior. I never forgot to pray that God would intervene for this child.

No one ever told me how a father was supposed to treat his child. Fathers should treat their children as human beings who deserve respect. A father caring for his family involves more than just providing food, shelter, and clothing. It also involves giving love, discipline, and time to family members. Children spell love as quality T-I-M-E. This is not merely time spent in the same house or room with them. This is T-I-M-E spent positively interacting with them.

> **And you, fathers, do not provoke your children to wrath, but bring them up in the training and admonition of the Lord.**
> **Ephesians 6:4**

One mother told me this about her ex-husband.

"He said that he was going to beat my son as many times as he could."

The child's grandmother overheard him make this statement.

She responded, "No you won't."

He never got a chance to abuse the child. The grandmother intervened and took the child to raise him.

The Word of God holds the father responsible for the discipline of the children. The father is to instruct and discipline the children, enforcing both his own and his wife's commands. The wife, on the other hand, as in other things, is the helpmate of her husband, and disciplines the children under the father's delegated authority, e.g., in his absence. No one ever told me that, and that is not what I had in mind.

In the dictionary, a father is a man who begets or raises a child. This nation has a host of fathers who are responsible and caring and their families are doing very well indeed. They love their wives and children and are loved in return. Many of them follow the teachings of Jesus who chose to identify God himself as the Heavenly Father.

And if you refuse to discipline your children, it proves you don't love them; if you love your children you will be prompt to discipline them.
Proverbs 13:24 NLT

At four years old, Cameron was in the front yard with his parents. A truck came around the corner. Although, the truck wasn't near either of his parents, Cameron screamed.
"Move Daddy!"

He forgot about his mother's safety. What caused him to have this amazing concern for his father's safety? Love was the motivating factor. Moreover, what has caused Cameron to love his father so? It's the Daddy's hugs, Daddy's kisses, and Daddy's love that he receives on a regular basis. His father knows the power of the Daddy's hugs, Daddy's kisses, and Daddy's love...

A son to my mother?
Is that what you expect from me?
Well, where was I supposed to learn that from?
Was she the one I was supposed to get my masculinity from?
She confused me with all her sensitivity...
My Daddy she could never be...
Who was the example to me?
I had no Daddy's hugs, no Daddy's kisses, and no Daddy's love...

A Son to my Mother?

The proverbs of Solomon. A wise son maketh a glad father: but a foolish son [is] the heaviness of his mother.
Proverbs 10:1

On January 3, 1983, after twenty-three hours of hard labor, I gave birth to a healthy baby boy, Herman Alexander Hall. His delivery was just the opposite of Earline's. I had informed the doctor that I wouldn't need anything for the pain. This was based on the smoothness of my previous delivery. Before the doctor made it down the hall, I was screaming for him to come back. At 4:06 P.M., the baby arrived weighing 7 lbs. 10 3/4 oz. I was in so much pain that I don't even remember when he arrived. I thought that I slept through it. He was named Herman, after my father. Alexander was my grandmother's last name. This was my miracle baby.

When my son was born, Robert was there. However, we were still separated. When I brought Herman home from the hospital, Robert stayed at the house a few days to help me out. I didn't want my child to look like his father or behave like his father. Eventually, I wanted to blot out every drop of his father's blood running through his veins. It was too late for that.

"We give more thought to who we marry than who we chose to have children with."
Earline Hall

Herman was exceptional from the very beginning. We never forgot that he was my miracle child. He gave us lots of reminders. The pregnancy had helped some of the physical problems in my body. My skin wasn't nearly as strained, and clothes weren't quite as irritating to my skin. After his birth, it was easier for me to stand almost erect. I wanted to breast feed my baby, and God blessed my chest just enough to perform this function. However, this area was still far short of normal.

When Herman was almost seven months old, I placed him in the living room floor on a blanket. I went outside to hang up the clothes. When I returned inside of the house, he was standing up at the living room table. A week later, Herman began walking. By the time he was a year old, he had a very large vocabulary of words. In addition, by the time he was eighteen months old, he could easily carry on an intelligible conversation. He developed one habit early. This habit would be very hard for him to break. He preferred to slip off from home, rather than ask for permission.

As Herman grew older, his escapades accelerated, almost beyond my ability to endure them. If I was expecting him to be a mild mannered child like Earline, I was sadly mistaken. I was dreadfully afraid that he might be like Robert. With a probing eye, I was always watching for any signs. I tried to be his mother and his father. He needed to be disciplined, but I wasn't about to let Robert discipline him. There were signs, but I couldn't interpret them.

He was warm and sensitive, and he idolized his older sister, Earline. Nevertheless, he wasn't like the mild mannered reserved Earline. He was strong-willed and was determined to do things his own way. Herman is also very warm, friendly, energetic, charming, and personable. The problem with his behavior was that his way of doing things was usually my wrong way. This child inherited all my excess baggage and many of my bad habits. At the time, I didn't know what was wrong with Herman. I was desperate to change his behavior.

There were constant calls from the schools about things that he was doing. He did very little to apply himself academically. All of my efforts to refine his behavior were unsuccessful and they were met with resistance. My love for Marijuana was passed on to him. There were times that it appeared that he hated me. He refused to come home at any decent hour, for years. His friends were the ones that break a mother's heart. It would have been easier if I could have said he was just like his father, but I refused to speak this curse over his life. In actuality, he was just like his mother.

Foolishness is bound up in the heart of a child, but the rod of correction will drive it far from him. Proverbs 22:15

He had inherited most of my bad habits, and all of my good habits. Wrestling with his behavior was like wresting with myself. Only, it took years for me to realize what was at the root of the problem. There were many times I was frustrated to the point of giving up.

When we think of a rod, we usually think of a physical or literal rod, i.e., a belt, switch, or strap. I tried using these with Herman, to no avail. All the traditional methods and many nontraditional methods of discipline failed. He refused to cry and repeated his behavior. He was always extremely mannerable and likeable. However, he was a force to be reckoned with when he felt challenged, crossed or threatened. Finally, after one of his escapades, I figured out what the real problem was.

My mother has a love for oriental rugs. One Saturday afternoon, she was nagging me about taking her to buy one of these rugs. Rather than doing this, I stopped to have my nails done. Not to be thwarted, she continued whining about the rug. This is just her way of getting her way. Finally, I told her that if she wasn't afraid, she would let Herman take her to pickup the rug. This was supposed to be a joke, because Herman had never driven a car in the road. Actually, he had only pulled a car into the driveway.

Herman asked me to give him the keys to the car. I gave them to him, still thinking that we were joking. Mama went out the door with him and got in the car. In my mind, surely, he wouldn't drive off in my car. To my utter dismay, Herman drove the car onto one of the busiest streets in Columbus. Mama had been driving for years, but was afraid to drive on this street.

Mama said when she told Herman to stop at the red light, he responded, "I've never done that."

They made it safely to the store, but Mama was realizing the danger that surrounded them. She told Herman to tell me to come pick her up, because she wasn't riding back to the nail salon with him. Mama was so scared that she had forgotten that she could drive. Realizing he was scared, too, reluctantly, she got back in the car, with Herman behind the steering wheel.

When they returned to the nail salon, Herman asked, "Where do you want me to park?"

Relieved that they had made it back safely, Mama responded, "Anywhere."

This experience caused me to look at Herman differently. This was something that I would have done if challenged. After all, his mother taught herself to drive. The problem was that he was just like me. He had inherited most of my bad habits, and all of my good habits. Wrestling with his behavior was like wresting with me. I realized that he was my child, and as such, he needed a lot of love. He needed to be accepted for who he was. I stopped trying to change him, and started working on accepting him. I needed a special rod of correction for him. This didn't mean that I liked the behavior. Nor did it mean that I stopped fussing. It simply meant that I had a better understanding of what I was working with. The traditional methods of discipline hadn't worked with me and they weren't working with him. Verbally, I began to say he was changing. My words began to speak blessings into his life.

A couple of months later, he got in trouble at school and I made a desperate decision to pull him out of school. Herman was in the ninth grade and showing no efforts to pass on to the tenth grade. The school district wanted to send him to the alternative school. I informed them that Herman wouldn't be returning to public school. A month later, I prepared to send him off to the Job Corps in North Carolina.

Not wanting to go, Herman said, "Mama I want to go back to school."

As I looked in to the eyes of my baby, I almost changed my mind, but I was resolved to do what was best for him.

Resolutely I told him, "You are my child but you don't have to make my mistakes."

This was the turning point for both of us. Rather than getting frustrated with his behavior, I began to deal with him the way I dealt with myself. Talking to him and punishing him wasn't going to work; he would have to learn from his own mistakes.

Herman arrived safely at the Job Corps, in spite of several adventures that he took during the bus trip. He wasn't prone to go directly anywhere and each time the bus would stop, he went exploring his surroundings. The week that he arrived at Job Corps, he went through diagnostic testing. He only missed one question out of all his tests. The next week, he passed the GED exam. Then I began arranging for him to come home to take the SAT. On his first weekend pass, I took him to a college in Atlanta where he made 1000 on the SAT. This was remarkable, since, he had never given any effort to learning anything, and hadn't completed the ninth grade. At sixteen, he began attending college in Atlanta, but all he wanted to do was collect telephone numbers. Later, I brought him back to Columbus. This was when the biggest battle for his soul took place.

Only take heed to thyself, and keep thy soul diligently, lest thou forget the things which thine eyes have seen, and lest they depart from thy heart all the days of thy life: but teach them thy sons, and thy son's sons;

especially the day that thou stoodest before the Lord thy God in Horeb, when the Lord said unto me, Gather me the people together, and I will make them hear my words, that they may learn to fear me all the days that they shall live upon the earth, and that they may teach their children. Deuteronomy 4:9-10

As God been to draw Herman, the devil began to fight to keep him. I was determined that he would not destroy my male child. As the battle intensified, we began to leave the radios in the house tuned to Christian stations twenty-four hours a day. We saturated the house with the Word and praise. I found the rod that I needed to bring about correction in his life. The rod of correction was the little member in my mouth. My tongue began to speak life to him. My words began to speak blessings into his life. Rather than speaking threats, I began to call him on the telephone to speak blessings in his life. At home, I constantly reminded him of who he was in Christ Jesus.

Herman had confessed salvation at age five, and the devil had fought him from that point on.

Mama said to God one day, "Lord, you have blessed me to witness to a lot of people, but I have never seen any of them get saved."

A few days later, on a Sunday morning, she walked into her bedroom and found Herman. He was on his knees leaning over the red velvet stool at the foot of the bed. He was engrossed in prayer. He never heard Mama enter the room. Herman had been listening to

Jimmy Swaggart on television. When the preacher made the call for salvation, Herman accepted the call.

When Mama came back into the room, she questioned Herman.

"Herman, what were you doing? Were you praying?"

"Yes Ma'am!"

"Were you saying what Jimmy Swaggart was saying on TV?"

"Yes Ma'am!"

"Herman, you're saved. You're not only my grandson; you're my brother in the Lord."

There was a battle from that point on. The battle intensified over the years. However, God gave me the rod that was needed for correction. This is how the rod brought about correction.

"Herman, do you know who you are?"

"Do you know that you are a handsome young man?"

"Do you know that you are a fine young man?"

"Do you know that you are going to make a wonderful father and husband?"

"Do you know that God is going to use you to travel the world and bring souls to Christ?"

"Do you know how many souls you are going to win for the Lord?"

"Do you know the anointing and call that God has placed upon your life?"

"Herman, do you know that you are going to be mightily used by God?"

"Do you know that you are the head and not the tail?"

"Do you know that you walk above and not beneath?"

"Do you know that you are the only Jesus some people will ever see?"

"Do you know that God has made choice of you?"

"Herman, do you know who you are?"

If he didn't know the answer to these questions, he found the answers. You would think that a child raised in the church almost from birth would have known who he was in Christ. He knew the Word. However, he needed to hear them spoken to him and reinforced in his life.

For years, I had spoken other words into his life. I never had a shortage of words. The other messages that he had heard from me were quite different.

"You hard headed disobedient child."

"You're the hard headiest child that I have ever met."

"Your head is harder than mine ever was."

"You see what I am going through. You see how you treat me. Your children are going to treat you worse."

"You are going to reap what you are sowing."

"I'm never going to keep your children."

"I'm only having one grandchild and I already have that one."

He calmly responded, "I'm never going to have children."

The rod of correction did what God said it would do. At eighteen, God beautifully saved Herman. Now at twenty, Herman is a soul winner and a prayer warrior. He's a member of the group *Anointed Disciples*. They sing gospel Rap but the messages are profound. He still has a beautiful sweet spirit. He's no longer afraid to have children. One day, he will marry and have his own family. I'll never excuse him for not being a *Real Man*. By the grace of God, he will never abuse his wife or walk away from his children. He didn't inherit his father's temperament or weaknesses. To the glory of God, those curses aren't lingering over his life. He's beautifully saved.

They will be My people, and I will be their God. I will give them singleness of heart and action, so that they will always fear Me for their own good and the good of their children after them. I will make an everlasting covenant with them: I will never stop doing good to them, and I will inspire them to fear Me, so that they will never turn away from Me. I will rejoice in doing them good and will assuredly plant them in this land with all My heart and soul. Jeremiah 32:38-41 NIV

To God belongs all the glory for what He has done in his life. I'll never be able to thank Him enough for setting my child free from the curse that I brought on his life.

Robert had his own issues, his own holes. He couldn't provide for Herman Daddy's hugs, Daddy's kisses, and Daddy's love... Robert has never beat or disciplined Herman. This was never an option. There was no way that I would ever have allowed the man who beat me to discipline my child. This was a factor that I should have considered before marrying him and allowing him to father my child. It is something that every person involved in an abusive relationship should consider.

As for Herman, he had no Daddy's hugs, no Daddy's kisses, and no Daddy's love... Nevertheless, he has found real Daddy's hugs, real Daddy's kisses, and real Daddy's love...

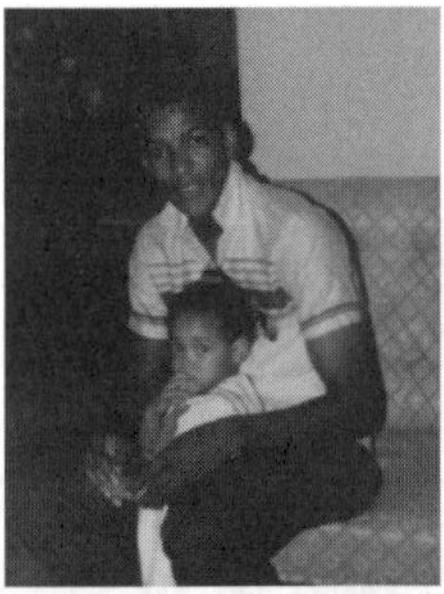

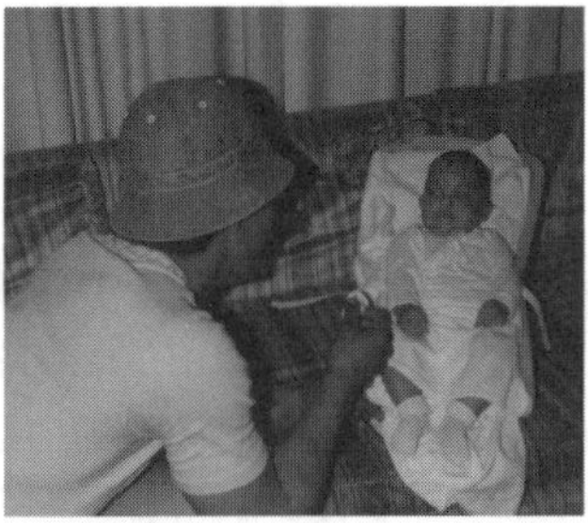

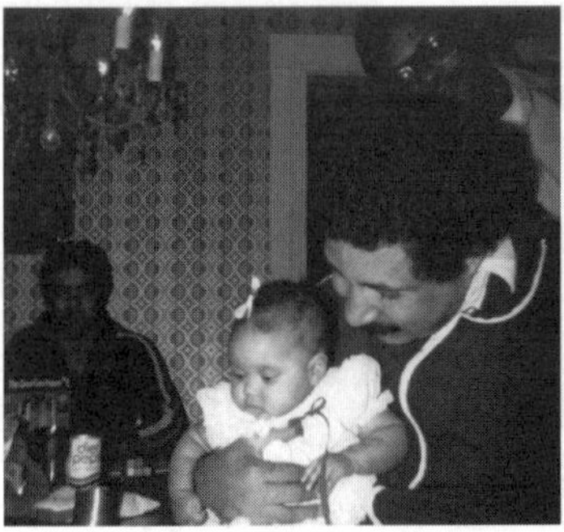

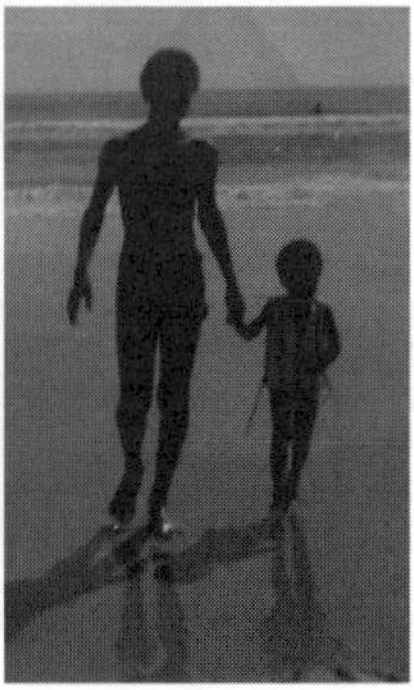

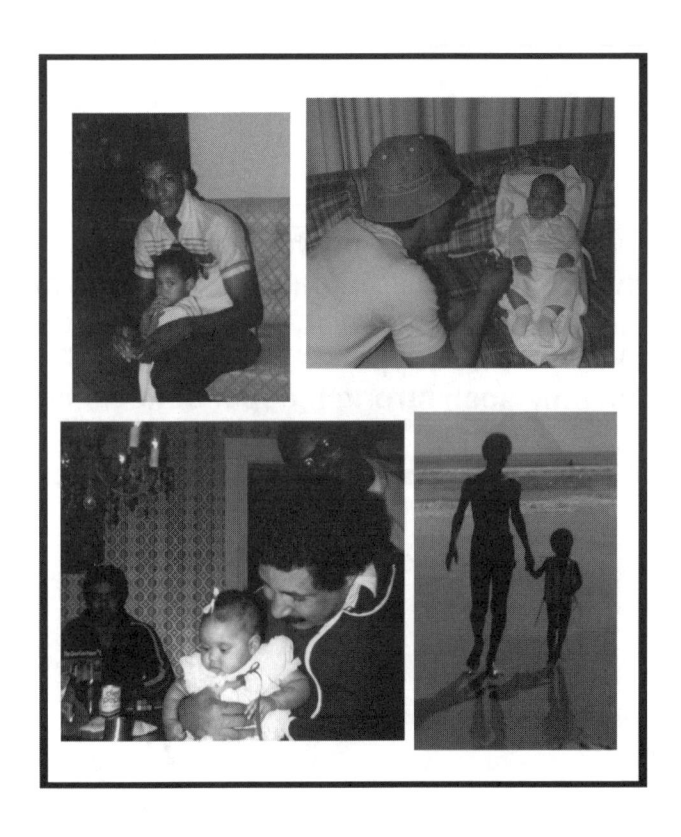

**A wife to my husband
Is that something you really expected of me?
Honor him, respect him, and support him?
What's that supposed to mean to me?
I have only seen strong independent women…
I don't have that identity…
Who was supposed to teach that to me?
I had no Daddy's hugs, no Daddy's kisses, and no Daddy's love…**

A Wife to my Husband?

My grandmother, Earline Alexander was born on October 6, 1920 and passed on January 13, 2000. She was the example of love, humility, giving, and patience, in word and deed. To her friends, she was known as Byrd. However, for me she was Ma'Dear. She gave us something more precious than gold, the gift of laughter. She taught us how to laugh at our mistakes, how to laugh at ourselves, and finally how to laugh in the midst of sorrow. When Ma'Dear was diagnosed with Alzheimer's, she maintained her sense of humor. Whenever she would become confused, she would turn it into a joke. When she was diagnosed with cancer, a month before her death, she showed no anger or resentment.

Now there was another side of Ma'Dear. There was one way to guarantee that it surfaced, hurt one of her children. My Uncle Carlton and I are three weeks apart. Growing up we were best friends. We did many things together. We began drinking and buying beer when we were around five years old. In the projects, there were several liquor houses. We knew all of the houses. We also knew which houses offered credit. One day, we decided that we wanted a beer. We told the woman that ran the house Ma'Dear wanted a beer on credit. Ma'Dear soon found out what we had done, but we had already drunk the beer.

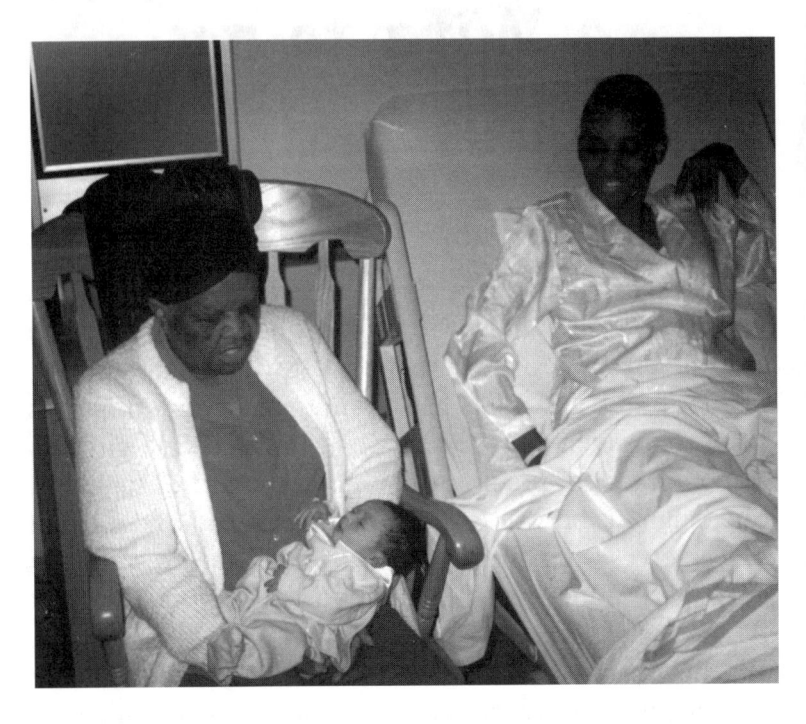

By the time we were in sixth grade, we were purchasing beer from the liquor store around the street. The first time they asked for identification was the week of my eighteenth birthday. By that time, we had been buying beer for years.

One of the neighbors would send Carlton to the store almost every day. She gave him some change for bringing the beer back. One day, she told Ma'Dear that Carlton didn't bring her the correct change. Things happened so fast that all we know is that Pickle (the fighter in the family) had to pull Ma'Dear off the woman. Ma'Dear had her on the ground in the back yard and she was getting ready to hit her in the head with a brick.

This wasn't the first time Ma'Dear went to bat for one of her children. My mother has always been easy going. One day, some girls followed Mama home from school. One of them wanted to fight Mama. Ma'Dear grabbed the child by the arm and the child ended up on the other side of the railroad track. You didn't mess with Ma'Dear's children.

Now, let me tell you about my mother. Mama has a very smart mouth. She inherited this from Ma'Dear. While in high school, Mama had a teacher who had a favorite saying.

"Don't give me that bologna."

One day, after the teacher made this statement, Mama responded.

"What do you want Souse Meat?"

She said this was not something that she had planned to say. She was extremely relieved that the other students kept her secret.

Who can find a virtuous and capable wife? She is worth more than precious rubies... Her husband can trust her, and she will greatly enrich his life. She will not hinder him but help him all of her life. She finds wool and flax and busily spins it. She is like a merchant's ship; she brings her food from afar off. She gets up before dawn to prepare breakfast for her household and plan the day's work for her servant girls. She goes out to inspect a field and buys it, with the earnings she plants a vineyard. She is energetic and strong, a hard worker. She watches for bargains; her lights burn late into the night. Her hands are busy spinning thread, her fingers twisting fibers. She extends a helping hand to the poor and opens her arms to the needy. She has no fear of winter for her household because all of them have warm clothes. She quilts her own bedspreads. She dresses like royalty in gowns

**of finest cloth. Her husband is well known, for he sits in the council meeting with the other civic leaders. She makes belted linen garments and sashes to sell the merchants. She is clothed with strength and dignity, and she laughs with no fear of the future. When she speaks her words are wise, and kindness is the rule when she gives instructions. She carefully watches all that goes on in her household and does not have to bear the consequences of laziness. Her children stand and bless her. Her husband praises her.
Proverbs 31:10-28 NLT**

Now, most of that scripture sounds like the kind of wife that I always wanted to be. I could cook, sew, crochet, embroider, and even repair the car on occasion. I knew how to provide for my family. Certainly, I had no problem with wearing fine clothes. Most of the time, my words were very encouraging to my husband. If you had asked me, I would have firmly declared that I was a virtuous woman. There were just a few things lacking. My wounds kept leaking on those around me. My own selfish needs kept resurfacing. I wasn't whole. As long as there remained a crack in my armor, I would never be what God called me to be to my family.

You wives will submit to your husbands as you do to the Lord. Eph. 5:22 NLT

The New Testament teaches that wives are to submit to their husbands. This is an extremely difficult responsibility for many wives to fulfill. It is hard to submit when there is no trust. When a woman has no father to trust, it becomes almost impossible for her to trust her husband. The pain that remains from the absence of her father will threaten to destroy her relationship with her husband. Submitting wasn't an active part of my vocabulary, and I was determined that it would not be apart of any relationship that I was involved in.

When I met Buck, I was vulnerable. I had wanted a good and solid relationship for years. He came along during one of the crisis periods in my life. I met him after years of struggles with Robert and Jim. I had been battered and bruised from the storm and the rain in my life. I had walked away from my relationship with God. I wanted someone to love me, but I had baggage, and baggage, and baggage.

When we met each other, some of the shallow holes (mild dysfunctions) began to fill, immediately. This led to a need for some serious readjustments. The strain of the adjustment caused the more severe holes (severe dysfunctions) to deepen and widen.

Eventually, we got married, and I wanted to be the Proverbs kind of wife. I just never saw that example. Our marriage started off crazy from the beginning. We both felt pressured to get married because it was obvious that I was going to prison. The state of Georgia has strict rules about ex-felons. We knew that it would be a problem for us to continue our relationship with me in prison and him on parole. Particularly, since we had been co-defendants on a previous case.

We had some kind of honeymoon, one that will never be forgotten. The suite wasn't exactly the executive suite or the penthouse. It was bunk with whomever you can until you can get a private room, or more appropriately, find a place to put your mattress on the floor of one of the cells. There was room service, but no choices from the menu. The food was passed through the flap in the wall. There was no private Jacuzzi. However, there was a public shower without doors. It had windows that faced the main hall. Anyone walking by could observe you bathing. Additionally, anyone sitting in the day room of the cell could observe the ritual. This was a point of contention for me, because people wanted to see my scars. There was no way that I was going to accommodate their desire. Rather than endure the humiliation, I took birdbaths in my room. There was no plush carpet but concrete floor. There was no down filled bed and satin sheets, but a metal bed with a thin twin plastic mattress. There were midnight chats, as the other inmates discussed how crazy I was to keep saying that I would be going home in a few months.

I spent the first two weeks of the honeymoon without my husband, communicating regularly through the mail. Before the end of the month, my new husband joined me for the honeymoon. However, he was not coming to share my suite. There was a separate suite reserved for him, with his name on it. He was assigned to the fifth floor, and I was housed on the third floor. He made arrangements to secure the room directly above mine. You see, the Muscogee County Jail has a rather unique communication system. Somehow, the toilets are connected between the floors. If you pumped the water in the toilet out and disinfected the toilet with Comet, newspaper could be used to make a kind of horn. The horn extended from the toilet allowing your voice to travel through the newspaper and through the pipes. Thus, you were able to talk between floors. This was how we spent our honeymoon, bent over the toilet talking to each other.

Buck had ignored all of my warnings to stop stealing. Nagging is probably more accurate. I had repeatedly warned him about one specific store. I had begged him not to go back there. This is where he was caught. I had dreamed that he would be caught soon in this store. Therefore, his arrest wasn't really a surprise to me. However, his being locked up made me really angry with him. Now, I didn't know when I would see him again. In addition, I had stood by him while he was incarcerated; he had a responsibility to do the same for me. Him standing by me was actually more of a fantasy that I had. I knew that drugs were his first love. Eventually, the drugs would interfere with anything that he was planning to do for me. I understood the hold the addiction had on his life.

Buck was calm about the whole thing, almost relieved that the suspense was over. My mind was torn now. The sooner that I was sent off to prison, the sooner I would be able to make parole. However, being sent off also meant that I wouldn't be able to talk to him or see him. He was my moral support during this ordeal. Talking to him helped keep me from dwelling on the length of my sentence. This had given us some time to do limited bonding.

This was a time when our friendship really developed. It was perhaps here that we began to develop our nonverbal communication skills. Hear me out. How can you develop nonverbal communication skills without looking at the person that you are communicating with? Because of the communication system at the jail, it was also possible for other people to hear portions of your conversations. If the toilet was pumped out on other floors in the line, it was as if having a party line (shared line).

The honeymoon lasted for a couple of months before I changed suites, and the extended honeymoon began. I was in the next group of women prisoners sent to Hardwick, Georgia. At this time, the only women's prison in the state was located in Hardwick.

Early one morning, the names were called of the people who were leaving in fifteen minutes for the prison in Hardwick. My name was one of about twelve names that were called. Hurriedly, I tried to wake Buck up so that I could say goodbye, while at the same time throwing my limited belongings into a pillowcase. About 6:30 A.M., we were shipped off to Hardwick. My heart was broken. I would miss him, greatly.

When I got to Hardwick, my nagging got worse. Nagging was going to be a routine part of our relationship for many years. I didn't know how to submit. I was comfortable being in charge. In my world, men had always been scarce. There were no positive male role models for me. You see I had no Daddy's hugs, no Daddy's kisses, and no Daddy's love...

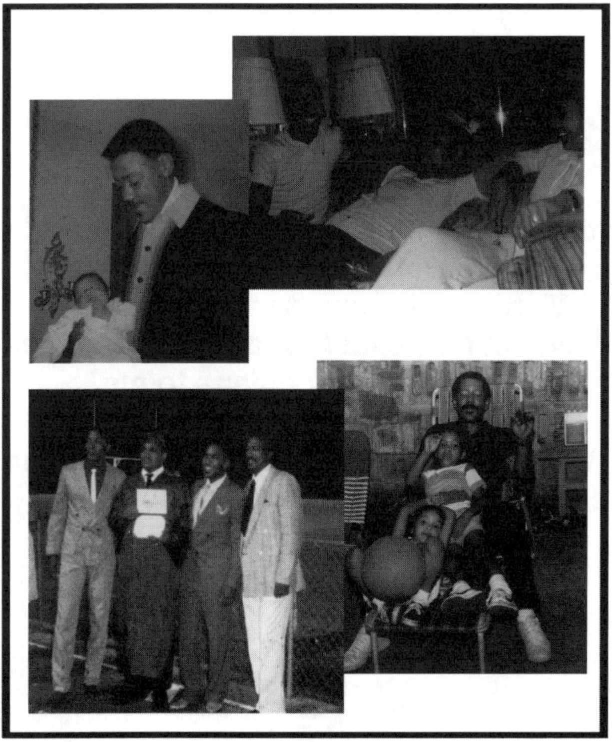

A husband to my wife?
Is that something you really expected of me?
Respect her, protect her, and be faithful to her…
What's that supposed to mean to me?
Neglect her, beat her, and cheat on her...
That's what it means to me…
I don't have that identity…
Who was supposed to teach that to me?
I had no Daddy's hugs, no Daddy's kisses, and no Daddy's love…

A Husband to my Wife?

**Husbands, love your wives, just as Christ also loved the church and gave himself up for her.
Ephesians 5:25**

In biblical times, the father was the undisputed head of the household. While some may have been authoritarian rulers, others were the compassionate anchors that held the family firmly together. The head of the household provided the discipline. Respect and honor was due the head of the household. He was responsible for overseeing spiritual matters for the family, for educating the children, teaching the sons a trade, administrating the business, buying and selling, and negotiating the marriage of his children.

I tried to engrave this in Buck's brain. I nagged him into reading Ephesians 5:25 over and over and over again. It didn't work. He loved me the way that he knew how to love. That had nothing to do with the way that Christ loved. Buck had missed that godly example. By the time he met me, he already had another love, drugs. I was his second choice and second love. He never owned up to this, but it was etched in my heart. He wanted me to come first, but he never had that example. On the other hand, I knew what I wanted from him, and I was not willing to be defeated easily, so I kept nagging.

Buck had his own holes that needed to be filled. He kept looking for answers in the drugs. This ultimately kept him revolving in and out of prison. While he was in prison, I had to be the head of the house. I was determined to be good at it, and I became comfortable in the role. Whenever Buck returned home, I wanted him to assume the role of the head of the house. However, I didn't know how to turn loose or step aside. My way was the right way, and I kept nagging him to get it right. This kept confusion in our family, and kept the cycle going. We were two halves that had joined together to make a quarter. Some people say that two halves make a whole, not in a marriage.

Too many holes needed filling. We were trying to be something that we didn't have a clue about how to become. There was a lot of growing that needed to be done in both of our lives. He didn't know how to love me, and I didn't know how to receive what he was trying to give me, his version of love. His love for the drugs kept me feeling insecure for years. I just couldn't compete with them. Finally, I decided to stop trying. We were both miserable. It seemed pointless to keep the relationship up. I wanted a husband but that's not what I was getting.

When I decided to end the marriage, the love was still there. I loved Buck and I knew that he loved me. Love just wasn't enough. We needed something stronger if the marriage was going to survive. It seemed to me that we didn't have what it was going to take to survive. Rather than nagging Buck, I began nagging God. No longer asking Him to deliver Buck, I was begging for permission to end the marriage. I remembered the vision that God had given me of Buck in the pulpit, but I wanted to forget it. He wasn't being consistent in His walk with God.

Enough was enough. There were too many issues. Too many holes needed to be filled. There was too much pain in the relationship for it to be salvaged. His drug usage had caused me a lot of pain. I had been faithful in responding with razor sharp words that pierced his heart. With my salvation, my words had taken on a new twist. I knew how to divide the scriptures to suit my needs. I kept condemning him with my words. I was too impatient and hurting too bad to wait for The Word to bring conviction. For years, I didn't understand the difference between condemnation and conviction.

Frustrated, I walked away from the man that I loved. I decided to let God have him, because I just couldn't handle any more. Buck prayed for God to intervene. He learned how to pray for his wife. There had to be a way to repair the damage of no Daddy's hugs, no Daddy's kisses, and no Daddy's love…

115

Faithful and true?
You must be kidding me.
Who was my example supposed to be?
Who was committed to me?
He said he was coming back….
Who was supposed to pick up the slack?
I had no Daddy's hugs, no Daddy's kisses, and no Daddy's love…

Faithful and True?

Fathers have the responsibility of teaching their children right and wrong, truth and error. They have the responsibility for teaching their children moral values, dependability, compassion, and responsibility. When the father walks away from his responsibilities, it sets the child up for failure in these areas. If the father is unfaithful, it enforces the acceptability of this behavior in the child.

Herman spent a lot of time with my Uncle Teddy when he was a toddler. Teddy liked to take Herman for long walks. Herman was short for his age, and he walked at seven months. These two factors together made him irresistible to women. Teddy used Herman to perfect his game. He used him to collect telephone numbers. Whenever Herman was with him, women stopped.

"Ooh! He's so cute."

This gave him a chance to ask for their telephone numbers. When Herman went off to college at sixteen, what did he do? He assumed that his sole purpose in being there was to collect telephone numbers. Actually, he started collecting numbers before he started college. Before he walked in salvation, he collected telephone numbers. There were numbers on paper plates, french-fries packages, paper bags, and anything else that he found handy. I wonder where he learned this habit.

A righteous man who walks in his integrity— how blessed are his sons after him.
Proverbs 20:7

To have a solid family, you must first have solid parents. Moreover, because the parents are to support the family, not only economically but also morally and spiritually, the family obviously should be established on a good foundation. I would love to say that my marriage was built on a firm foundation. However, that would be a lie. It was built on holes and bleeding wounds.

Lord and King, you are God! Your words can be trusted. You have promised many good things to me. 2 Samuel 7:28

My first and second marriages were plagued by infidelity. It would be easy to point fingers and lay blame. My first marriage hardly qualifies as a marriage or a relationship. Therefore, I will not even discuss that farce. However, I will discuss my marriage to Buck, who is now Henry.

Buck and I have loved each other almost from the time we met. Should we say, "Love at first sight" or was it "lust at first sight?" Surely, love was enough to keep us faithful and true. It would be easy to say he did, and I only did, or it was only because of this and that. There are many excuses, and for years, I blamed him for all the problems in our marriage. Rather than elaborating on the gory details, I'll just say that our wounds bled on each other. Selfish love doesn't know how to be faithful and true. Drugs, insecurity, deceit, egos, revenge, and hidden hurts were contributing factors. When you trace it back to the root, it sings the same song; "we had no Daddy's hugs, no Daddy's kisses, and no Daddy's love…"

Help me, O LORD my God! Save me because of your unfailing love. Psalms 109:26 NLT

For years, I begged God to let me divorce Buck. After all, I had cause. He had cause. It didn't matter that infidelity wasn't the reason that I was seeking a divorce. I couldn't prove that he had been unfaithful, but we had shared many of our shortcomings. The vows had been violated. You see we were also friends, and sometimes the secrets were difficult to keep. When it was all said and done, I really didn't have to worry about a woman taking my place in his life, and he definitely didn't have to worry about another man stealing my heart. I only wanted one man, Buck. Nevertheless, things kept happening, and I kept begging God to let me out of the relationship. I was tired of the lifestyle, drugs and prison. The revolving cycle seemed from my point of view to be endless.

Consider Jesus' reply to the Pharisees. I knew this scripture well. Reading it repeatedly, I found cause for divorce, not a commandment for divorce. There was always the choice of forgiveness. It seemed to me that you could forgive and still get a divorce.

The Pharisees also came unto Him, tempting Him, and saying unto Him, Is it lawful for a man to put away his wife for every cause? And He [Jesus] answered and said unto them, Have ye not read, that He which made them at the beginning made them male and female, And said, For this cause shall a man leave father and mother, and shall cleave to his wife: and they two shall be one flesh? Wherefore they are no more two, but one flesh. What therefore God has joined together, let not man put asunder. They say unto Him, Why did Moses then command to give a writing of divorcement, and to put her away? He said unto them, Moses, because of the hardness of your hearts, allowed you to put away your wives: but from the beginning it was not so. And I say unto you, Whosoever shall put away his wife, except it be for fornication, and shall marry another,

committeth adultery: and whoso marrieth her
which is put away doth commit adultery.
Matthew 19:3-9

Today, many couples divorce for practically any reason, and then remarry. Some authorities even allow what is called "no fault divorce," which makes divorcing one's spouse quite "effortless." However, according to God's word they could well be permitting adultery.

In the Apostle Paul's letter to the church at Ephesus, he gives solid advice to husbands and wives on the subject of divorce.

Wives, submit yourselves unto your own husbands, as unto the Lord. For the husband is the head of the wife, even as Christ is the head of the church: and He is the Savior of the body. Therefore as the church is subject unto Christ, so let the wives be to their own husbands in everything. Husbands, love your wives, even as Christ also loved the church, and gave Himself for it, that He might sanctify and cleanse it with the washing of water by the word, that He might present it to Himself a glorious church, not having spot, or wrinkle, or any such thing, but that it should be without blemish. So ought men to love their wives as their own bodies.

He that loveth his wife loveth himself. For no man ever yet hated his own flesh; but nourisheth and cherisheth it, even as the Lord the church. For we are members of His body, of His flesh, and of His bones. For this cause shall a man leave his father and mother. And shall be joined unto his wife, and they two shall be one flesh. This is a great mystery: but I speak concerning Christ and the church. Ephesians 5:22-32

Paul was writing about the type of relationship that a husband and wife should have with each other. He wrote that wives should submit themselves to their husbands in all things. He further explains that the husbands should love their wives, as Christ loved the church, even sacrificing himself for it. I reasoned that if Buck loved me as Christ loved the church, I would have no problem submitting to him. Since he didn't love me like that, there was no reason for me to submit. I didn't tell him, but whenever he gave me a choice or failed to give me clear guidelines, I did it Charlotte's way. Whenever, he gave me a clear directive, I did exactly what he said, because I was mindful of this scripture. There was one problem; Buck's normal way of communicating with me always allowed me a way of escape. Normally, I took the way of escape.

Here's an example of my manipulative behavior. Buck had started using drugs again. The next step to follow was for me to put him out the house. To be more exact, I couldn't put him out the house. However, I could put his clothes out and nag him to follow the clothes. During one of these periods, I celebrated my birthday. He is never prone to miss celebrating or acknowledging any special occasions. This one would be no different. He took me out to lunch, but I could tell he was very impatient. He was ready for the date to be over so that he could get on with his daily activities. To be honest, that "monkey" on his back was giving him a fit, the drug addiction. We had an argument and lunch ended abruptly. We were expecting a large check at the end of the week. Well, the check came that day. The next morning, I went on a shopping spree and spent the whole check. The day the check was supposed to arrive, Buck called me.

"CJ, did the check come today?"

"No Buck, it didn't come today."

A few days later, he came by the house. When he saw all the new furniture, he smiled and said, "I know my wife."

By this time, I was no longer angry and I was looking for a way to tell him that I had spent the check. Relieved, I responded, "What do you know about your wife?"

"She loves to shop."

"And what else?"

He hadn't figured out what he needed to know about me. Whenever, I was upset, I went shopping. For over a month, he called every day and repeated his question

"CJ, did the check come today?"

"No Buck, it didn't come today."

Finally, he called and said, "CJ, did the check come any day?"

"Yes, Buck."
"When did the check come?"
"On my birthday."
"What happened to the check?"
"I bought the furniture. I thought that you would figure it out when you said that you knew me."

From the beginning of our relationship, we had established a rule that we would never go to bed angry with each other. We did not always adhere to the rule, but we were never prone to be angry with each other for an extended period. Most of the time, our differences were resolved before we went to bed. This time, he wanted to be angry with me, but that's not his nature. In a couple of days, he decided to come back home. He had actually forgiven me before I admitted what I had done. He knew that I never wasted money. If I had blown the money recklessly, perhaps the outcome would have been different. In recent months, I have come to realize that he loves me unconditionally. After all, love is supposed to be unconditional. This kind of love is only possible when

Christ is at the center of the marriage. Moreover, yes, the love is reciprocal.

We also know that the Son of God has come. He has given us understanding. Now we can know the One who is true. And we belong to the One who is true. We also belong to His Son, Jesus Christ. He is the true God. He is eternal life. 1 John 5:20 NLT

The strong permanent bond of love that Christ has for the church, and vice versa, typifies the kind of bond that husbands and wives should have for each other. The focal point of the marriage relationship is Christ! This scripture bears repeating.

For we are members of His [Christ's] flesh, and of His bones, For this cause shall a man leave his father and mother, and shall be joined unto his wife, and they two shall be one flesh. Eph. 5:30-31

A respectable member of society?
Now please define that for me?
All I know is what I see on TV....
Crime, murder, hatred, and drugs are all around me...
Now you tell me not believe what I see?
You must be kidding me.
It's my environment that I see....
Who was supposed to provide for me?
I had no Daddy's hugs, no Daddy's kisses, and no Daddy's love...

A Respectable Member of Society?

Understand, therefore, that the LORD your God is indeed God. He is the faithful God who keeps His covenant for a thousand generations and constantly loves those who love Him and obey His commands.
Deuteronomy 7:9

Is the family structure important to the well-being of our society? Is the family important to God? Is there a relationship between husband and wife resembling that between Christ and his church? Where are children taught values? Whose responsibility is it to teach children how to become productive members of society?

Delinquency, youth violence, gangs, early sexual involvement, alcohol and drug abuse and other problem behaviors in our young people are causes for grave concern in this country. Concern for the values and morals of the young are an enduring adult preoccupation. Down through recorded history, this worry about the character of the younger generation is evident. Concern, however, has never been enough to ensure that the children possess the type of character that can sustain the individual and society. Some families have failed to transmit their values to their young children. Many parents have failed to understand the seriousness of the responsibility that God has entrusted to them.

> **He remembered our utter weakness.**
> **His faithful love endures forever.**
> **Psalms 136:23 NLT**

It has often been said, "A chain is only as strong as its weakest link." If this theory holds true then a family or society is only as strong as its weakest link. If we were to look at the various components that make up our society and refer to them as links, we would see that one of the most vital links in the chain is that of the family unit. It appears that link has been greatly weakened.

> **And you shall teach [God's commandments] to your sons, talking of them when you sit in your house and when you walk along the road and when you lie down and when you rise up.**
> **Deuteronomy 11:19**

La'Toya's favorite thing about Grand Daddy Buck is the way that he carried her as a child. While I was in college, Buck usually kept La'Toya. Some days, Buck went on long walks with her. He would let her ride around his neck, as he carried the diaper bag in his hand.

If we examine the number of families that have been divorced, all the one-parent families, all the people living together without being married, and all the gay and lesbian partners, the total would be staggering. God instituted marriage, very soon after He created humanity. Marriage is something that God considers sacred, holy and permanent. However, in today's society people pay little attention to God's instructions for marital relationships. From the following verses, it can be clearly seen that God has established heterosexual marriage relationships.

And the rib, which the Lord had taken from man, made He a woman, and brought her unto the man. And Adam said, This is now bone of my bones, and flesh of my flesh: she shall be called Woman, because she was taken out of

Man. Therefore shall a man leave his father and his mother, and shall cleave unto his wife: and they shall be one flesh. Genesis 2:22-24

God structured the family unit in the same fashion that He structured the relationship of the church with Christ. God instituted the family structure. The family is a vital link in the chain that makes a solid society. If Satan succeeds in destroying the family structure and the sacredness of marriage, then society as we know it will be destroyed, also.

After one of my fights with Buck, I dropped his clothes off at his mother's house. Earline and Herman were in the car with me. Mama's house was the next stop. There I dropped the children off. I was so upset that I never noticed their feelings. Earline said that they couldn't forget the look on his face. They had Mama take them back to his mother's house. They wanted to be with him. They were afraid that they would never see him again. Later, he took them back to Mama. They agreed that they would never tell me.

Therefore shall ye lay up these words in your heart and in your soul, and bind them for a sign upon your hand, that they may be as frontlets between your eyes. And ye shall teach them your children, speaking of them when thou sittest in thine house, and when thou walketh by the way, when thou liest down, and when thou risest up.
Deuteronomy 11:18-20

The easiest groups of people to identify as Christian educators are Christian parents. They are all called to teach their children. No Christian parent is exempt from teaching the knowledge of God in their households. It would be a shame for a parent to lack proficiency at this calling in their home. The father should teach the civic and moral values widely held in our society, such as honesty, caring, dependability, fairness, trustworthiness, and integrity.

What the children learned from Buck was that it was acceptable to have fun. Here's what they say about him.

Earline says, "It was always easy to talk to him. He's just Buck."

La'Toya says, "I have always loved him. I just do. He's good to me."

From my niece, Courtney, "I remember him taking all of us to Discovery Zone and skating. He taught me how to skate."

With Ashley, "He rubbed my ears."

Tahee and Toronto remember Buck taking them to church. Afterward, he took them and La'Toya to the park.

From Tahee, "We had real fun. Uncle Buck bought us the biggest ice cream cones and Slushees."

Darlene said, "He taught me how to survive in the streets. He didn't want me there, but once I was out there, he taught me what I needed to know."

In addition, from Herman, "He remembered the exact Robo cop that I wanted. Whenever, Mama would be trying to beat me, he would talk to me. Sometimes, he would take me and leave the house. He let me sit in his lap and drive the car when I was in the second grade. His hands were nowhere near the steering wheel. However, he kept his foot on the pedals. He let me steer the wheel by myself. He tried to tell me about girls. I already knew about them but at least he tried. He didn't baby me. He treated me like a big kid. He let me punch him as hard as I could. He never lied to me. He's been straight up with me. He didn't treat me like a stepson."

When Herman was smaller, his name for Buck was "Buck Daddy" or "Daddy Buck." Now, he calls him just Buck. He called Herman, Joe Kid. Now, Buck calls Herman, Joe.

Earline also remembers Buck's attempt to teach her to drive.

"It lasted about five minutes. By the time I made two turns, the police pulled me over. I had turned right in front of the police. Buck was in the car behind me and he explained what was going on. The next time he let me drive, I hit the picnic table."

Brandon remembers, "Uncle Buck was the first person to take me bowling. He took Herman and me. This was important for me because it was the first time that I spent time with him."

Just as a father has compassion on his children, so the Lord has compassion on those who fear Him. Psalm 103:13 NLT

Several years ago, we took the children and Mama to Disney Land. Mama and I watched as the kids enjoyed the rides. Buck was on every ride with them. On one ride, Splash Mountain, they came down a real steep incline. We watched as they screamed and Buck covered

La'Toya's eyes. When they came off the ride, she wanted to set the record straight.

"I want to ride it again. I was trying to see but Grand Daddy Buck covered my eyes. He was the one scared."

La'Toya wanted to ride every ride in the park. However, there were some rides that she couldn't get the dare devil Herman or Grand Daddy Buck on.

When I asked one youth what was his favorite memory of his father, he thought about it for almost an hour before responding.

"One time, he bought me an outfit."

Quentin remembers his Grand Daddy.

"It was the times that we spent together, walking across the grass taking the trash out. Those times were special. He would talk to me. We could talk about anything. He loved to tell jokes."

I would be remiss, if I didn't mention Charlie C. Walker. He was the one that filled some of my gaps. When I was pregnant with Herman, he cooked chitterlings for me. However, the most important thing that he did for me was providing a sense of security. When I went to New York broke, he told me that he would send for me if I needed to come back home.

In the course of writing this section of the book, I talked to a number of mothers and children. Some said they had no meaningful memories or the memories may have been too painful to bear. While doing a book signing at store located next to a photo studio, I watched as a continuous stream of people patronized the store. This gave me an idea; it would be a perfect opportunity to gather pictures for the book. Men were frequently accompanying the children and their mothers into the studio. I had almost given up when I found one mother that had a picture with the father in it. Take time to make memories with the children.

An example for me?
How can this be?
Please explain that to me?
I had no Daddy's hugs, no Daddy's kisses, and no Daddy's love...
You say there is one who knows how to love me?
How can He love a failure like me?
He loves me so much that He died for me?
You mean there is one who cares about me?
He'll give me Daddy's hugs, Daddy's kisses, and Daddy's love...

An Example for Me?

**What would the IDEAL Daddy be?
A Daddy who loves the Word of God and loves the Lord with all his heart, all his soul and all his mind. He would love his wife as Christ loves the Church. He would love his family UNCONDITIONALLY and would
".... provoke not your children to wrath: but bring them up in the nurture and admonition of the Lord." Ephesians 6:4**

A couple years ago, as we celebrated the Christmas holidays, La'Toya was just a little upset. La'Toya was four years old. This year, she wanted a special doll. Earline had called stores all over Georgia looking for the doll, to no avail. La'Toya's father had also agreed to get the doll. We weren't taking any chances, so we looked for the doll, until time ran out. On Christmas Eve, Earline explained to the child's father that we opened presents at our house just after midnight. He said that he had the doll, and we begged him to bring it over. He became irate and adamantly refused. Earline asked if he could bring the toy on Christmas morning. He stated that whenever he brought the toy, she had better be happy to get it. He refused to let anyone know when he would bring the toy. Earline was upset. It was the only thing that La'Toya wanted that she had not been able to find. She even offered to pay him for the doll. She was so upset that I tried to reason with him. He became extremely nasty and I discontinued the conversation.

The next day, he came over to my house with two of his friends. He brought a bicycle and the doll. The doll was beautifully gift-wrapped. La'Toya was the wrong child to play games with. She had received another bicycle from Buck. She really wanted that one. When her father came in, she barely acknowledged him. He gave her the gift-wrapped doll. She hesitantly took the package and then laid it to the side. She never stopped playing with what she was playing with. We begged her to open the box.

After several minutes, she reached over, pulled the ribbon from the box, and stated, "I'll just take the bow off."

However, the box was left unopened. It took several more minutes of prodding and pleading to get her to open the box. When she finally opened it, she looked at the doll.

"Uh Amazing Amy."

Then as if she had never been interested in the doll, she laid the doll back to the side. We were embarrassed. She was so cold towards the present that it appeared she was acting out a script. It was several days later that she told her mother the truth.

After asking La'Toya had she changed her mind about the doll, she said "No I love Amazing Amy and was so happy when I got her for Christmas. I just didn't want my dad to know I wanted the doll so bad."

When asked why, she said, "I heard him talking to you on the telephone about the doll. I was in the other room eavesdropping on the telephone so that I could hear what I was getting for Christmas."

Last Christmas, La'Toya father called two days before and told her that he was going to get her something for Christmas. He asked her what she wanted, and she said that she didn't know.

She later said, "I would have been happy with anything because it is the thought that counts."

The next day he called and told her that he would give her a present the day after Christmas. Christmas day, he called again. La'Toya asked him about a present. According to La'Toya, he had a real fatherly response.

"I talked to Child Support Enforcement and they said that if I pay child support, I am not required to buy you anything for Christmas."

La'Toya said to her mother, "I felt like I was ready to pimp slap him."

She was upset that he kept changing his story. She was hurt that he did not think about how his words would make her feel.

Paul tells husbands to love their wives as Christ has loved His Church (Eph. 5:25), and for fathers to avoid "provoking their children to wrath" (Eph. 6:4). Surely, not all households during his time were so harmonious and compatible. Nevertheless, scriptural precepts, strong extended family relationships, and a family-oriented society give every opportunity for one.

The comforting side of all this is that we, who have trusted Christ as our Savior, have a Daddy who is worthy of all honors, all glory, and all praise. He is the Father who will never leave us nor forsake us. He is the Father whose love knows no limits, whose forgiveness knows no ends. He's the Daddy who never made a mistake and never will. He is the Daddy who understands our every weakness. The Daddy who has given us the best that He had to offer, sacrificing His own sinless Son for our sins. He has a perfect plan for us and provides all that we will ever need in this life and the life to come. Our Daddy in heaven will never let us down. Now, there is a Daddy worthy of being honored.

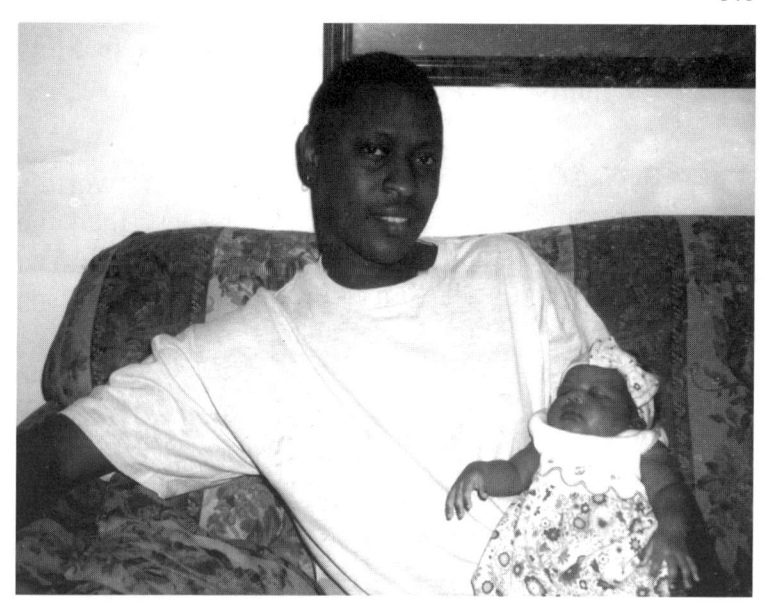

Earthly fathers should be reflections of our Heavenly Father. Every child wants a Daddy that he or she can look up to, maybe set on his lap, share the day with him and just know he will be there when we need him. For those not so blessed, there is a Father who is always there for us. He never judges us, and loves us more than anyone. Daddies who are generous, care deeply for their wives and children, rejoice when the children learn from their mistakes, and express their affection freely are a valuable asset to any family. If you ask them, you will also find that the majority of them get their strength from the relationship that they enjoy with their Heavenly Father, the perfect Daddy.

For our earthly fathers disciplined us for a few years, doing the best they knew how. But God's discipline is always right and good

for us because it means we will share in His holiness. Hebrews 12:10 NLT

Because the role of father is one of the world's most important roles of all time, Jesus described the traits of the ideal father, in what is generally called "The Story of the Prodigal Son." In this passage, Jesus describes the traits of the ideal father.

To illustrate the point further, Jesus told them this story: "A man had two sons. The younger son told his father, 'I want my share of your estate now, instead of waiting until you die.' So his father agreed to divide his wealth between his sons. A few days later this younger son packed all his belongings and took a trip to a distant land, and there he wasted all his money on wild living. About the time his money ran out, a great famine swept over the land, and he began to starve. He persuaded a local farmer to hire him to feed his pigs. The boy became so hungry that even the pods he was feeding the pigs looked good to him. But no one gave him anything. When he finally came to his senses, he said to himself, 'At home even the hired men have food enough to spare, and here I am, dying of hunger! I will go home to my father and say,

"Father, I have sinned against both heaven and you, and I am no longer worthy of being called your son. Please take me on as a hired man.'" "So he returned home to his father. And while he was still a long distance away, his father saw him coming. Filled with love and compassion, he ran to his son, embraced him, and kissed him. His son said to him, 'Father, I have sinned against both heaven and you, and I am no longer worthy of being called your son.' But his father said to the servants, 'Quick! Bring the finest robe in the house and put it on him. Get a ring for his finger, and sandals for his feet. And kill the calf we have been fattening in the pen. We must celebrate with a feast, for this son of mine was dead and has now returned to life. He was lost, but now he is found.' So the party began."

Luke 15:11-24 NLT

It is obvious that Jesus is identifying the father as God and the wayward son as each one of us, His disobedient children. The traits of the father in the story are outlined as follows:

- He is a good provider for his family and has enough material possessions with which to care for his family.

- He had a charitable spirit, generously giving to his son before his own death.
- He had a deep distress for the well-being of his son who chose to take his wealth and leave home for riotous living.
- He was a forgiving father who accepted his wayward son, now bankrupt and apologetic, back into the family circle.

- A loving father, who eagerly ran to his son, gave him Daddy's hugs, Daddy's kisses, and Daddy's love.
- He was an excited father, who held a banquet to celebrate his son's return home.

Today, we have an urgent need for more fathers who fulfill their roles after the example of the Heavenly Father.

A good man leaveth an inheritance to his children's children: and the wealth of the sinner is laid up for the just. Proverbs 13:22

Our Heavenly Father provides us with material resources. He gives us the freedom to use everything that he has provided. He is concerned for our well-being more deeply than we can ever conceive. He forgives us when we repent of our numerous mistakes. He accepts us graciously back into full fellowship with Him and His family. He blesses us every day with his unconditional agape love full of Daddy's hugs, Daddy's kisses, and Daddy's love.

Knowing who God is makes all the difference in our lives. Your children won't desire to know and draw near to God if they don't believe that He loves them unconditionally. They need to know that they can trust Him completely, and that He will take care of all their essential needs. It is God who gives sustenance, spiritual and emotional health, and confidence to face the trials that life brings. God gives us the grace to endure our trials, the courage to change the things that we can, and wisdom to deal with the things that we can't change.

To this you were called, because Christ suffered for you, leaving you an example that you should follow in His steps. He committed no sin, and no deceit was found in His mouth. When they hurled their insults at Him, He did not retaliate; when He suffered, He made no threats. 1 Peter 2:21-23 NIV

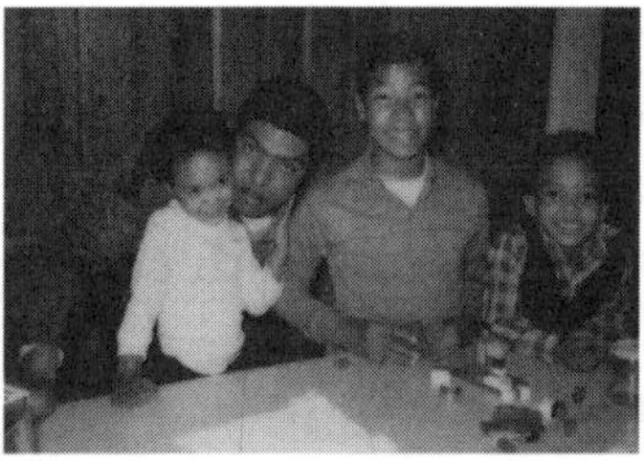

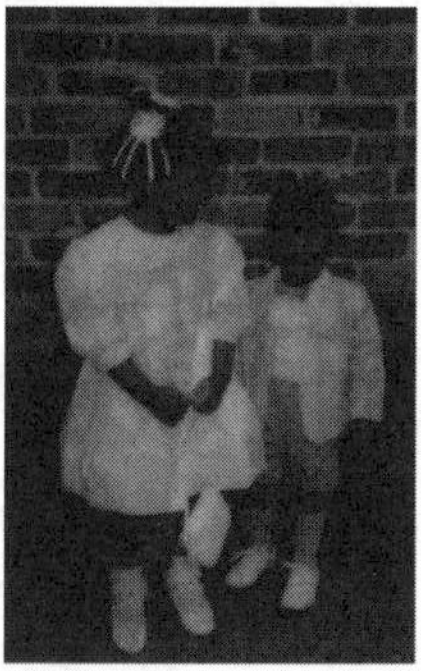

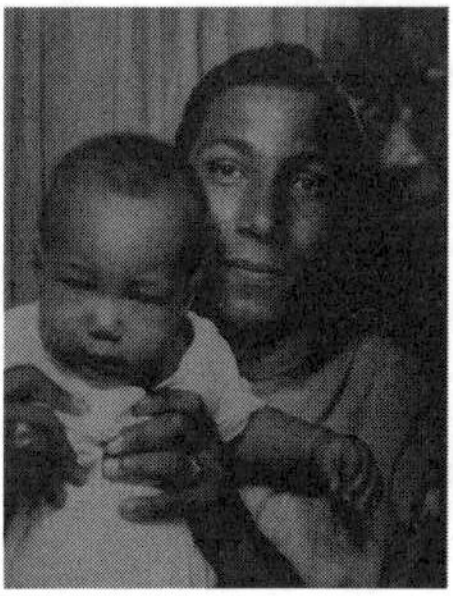

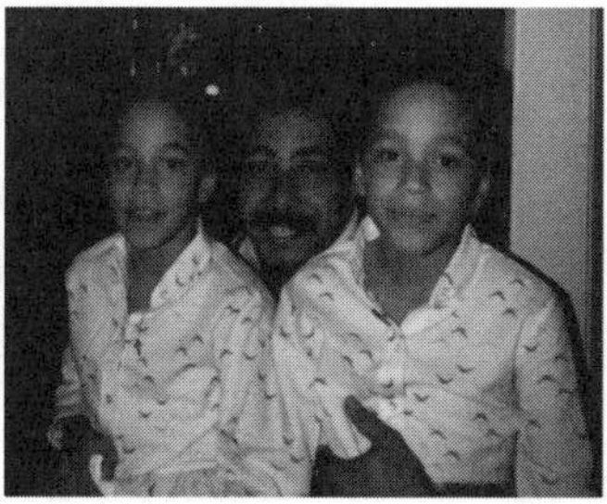

Rise up ye men of valor…
Rise up and take a stand…
Rise up and tear down the walls…
Walls of bitterness, walls of deceit…

Tear down those strongholds…
Tear down those oppressions…
Tear down the ruins…
Generational curses, generational trends…

Empower your children…
Empower your sons…
Empower your daughters…
To hear God's call…

The Charge

This charge comes to you now; rise up to take your children back. Reclaim what the thief has desired to steal from you. Step up and take charge of your household. Defy the odds. Defy the statistics. Be what God has called you to be, a man of honor, a man of integrity, a man of dignity, a man of valor, the spiritual head of your household, *a Real Man*, and a real Daddy. Stop settling for what statistics have branded you to be. Take charge of your destiny. Take charge of your family's future. Make the only choice for *Real Men*, the choice to let the perfect Daddy guide you. Ask Him today to order your steps according to His word. Ask Him to teach you how to be Daddy. Ask Him how to provide Daddy's hugs, Daddy's kisses, and Daddy's love.

But when the Holy Spirit controls our lives, He will produce this kind of fruit in us: love, joy, peace, patience, kindness, goodness, faithfulness, gentleness, and self-control. Here there is no conflict with the law.
Galatians 5:22-23 NLT

Let the significance of your relationship with God be on permanent display. Your children need to know that your decisions and actions are based on the Word of God. Don't just tell your children about God, model godly behavior. Let them see God working in your life. Show them that God is real in your life. Let them observe you praying and reading the Bible regularly. Talk naturally and casually with God and about your relationship with God. Share with them what you are learning from Him and how He is working in your life. Let your love of God be apparent. By demonstrating how God is the foundation for your life, you will establish a solid, positive foundation for your children's attitude toward God.

Several years ago, at age eleven Ashley joined the church. When asked why by the pastor, she shocked the church. She was standing at the front of the church, after the pastor extended the invitation.

The pastor asked, "Young lady are you coming forward because you want to be with Jesus?"

Ashley responded, "I want to be with my Daddy."

My children, listen to Me. Listen to your father's instruction. Pay attention and grow wise, Proverbs 4:1 NLT

Lead your children in prayer as you continually go to God to help you solve problems and care for your family. Make it an ordinary thing to stop and pray when you are trying to solve a problem, choose meals, or making purchasing decisions. Go to God when you are making family decisions, such as buying a new home or car, choosing a church home, or deciding where to go on vacation. Allow God to lead you when making life-changing decisions, like deciding which college your child should attend, or looking for a new job.

**With unfailing love You will lead
this people whom You have ransomed.
You will guide them in Your strength
to the place where Your holiness dwells.
Exodus 15:13**

Brandon remembers a time when Tyron took him to baseball game. It was just the two of them. This was a surprise for him. His Daddy made sure that he had everything that he wanted. It was important to Tyron that Brandon enjoyed himself.

Additionally, Brandon has severe asthma. He remembers the numerous times that his father took him to the emergency room and made sure that he took his medicine.

According to Brandon, "This meant that he cared."

Let your children be part of the decision-making process. Involve God anytime you are giving or receiving advice, and disciplining your children. A father's wisdom is to be shared with the children.

Moreover, this charge comes as an exhortation for those who have hidden wounds, hurts, and holes needing to be filled. Won't you be honest with Daddy today? Take charge of the pain. Take charge of the hurt. Don't let the wounds of the past destroy your potential. He's waiting to heal your heart. Let a Real Man, a Real Daddy heal the hurt. His arms are open wide. Won't you come?

Hear, ye children, the instruction of a father, and attend to know understanding. For I give you good doctrine, forsake ye not my law. For I was my father's son, tender and

only [beloved] in the sight of my mother. He taught me also, and said unto me, Let thine heart retain my words: keep my commandments, and live. Get wisdom, get understanding: forget [it] not; neither decline from the words of my mouth. Forsake her not, and she shall preserve thee: love her, and she shall keep thee. Wisdom [is] the principal thing; [therefore] get wisdom: and with all thy getting get understanding. Exalt her, and she shall promote thee: she shall bring thee to honour, when thou dost embrace her. She shall give to thine head an ornament of grace: a crown of glory shall she deliver to thee. Proverbs 4:1-9

No correction or discipline seems desirable when it is being received. However, the results can be life changing. Allow God to discipline and correct your behavior. This, can in turn, be passed on to your children. The fruits of righteousness will be the reward.

My son, despise not the chastening of the LORD; neither be weary of His correction. For whom the LORD loveth He correcteth; even as a father the son [in whom] he delighteth. Proverbs 3:11-12

On the other hand, children have a right to receive Daddy's hugs, Daddy's kisses, and Daddy's love. The children are commanded to be obedient to the parents. This is not license for cruel or inhuman treatment by parents, for the Bible adds the qualifying phrase, "In the Lord." Children have the right to expect reasonable direction and guidance from their parents, and the parents are called upon to nurture their children. That is, to rear them, to bring them up, in the "chastening and admonition of the Lord". That final phrase means that the parents are to imitate God as much as possible in the admonishing or urging given to the children, and also to imitate God in punishing when such becomes necessary. It is chastening or punishing based upon love, not revenge, upon caring, not indifference, upon betterment, not defilement.

My Daddy Helps Me
Original Author Unknown

Sung to: "My Bonnie Lies Over the Ocean"
My Daddy helps me when I'm sick.
My Daddy helps me when I'm blue.
My Daddy helps me when I'm sad.
Thanks, Dad, for all that you do!
You help, you help,
You help me feel so much better.
You help, you help,
You help me feel so much better.

155

**Well, Daddy it seems I have failed at everything
I have tried to be.
I need Daddy's hugs,
I need Daddy's kisses,
I need Daddy's love,
Dear God, I long to be free.
Can You help me to be what You would have me
to be?**

Father Help Me!

But if we confess our sins to Him, He is faithful and just to forgive us and to cleanse us from every wrong.
1 John 1:9 NLT

Recently, one of my friends related this to me.
"I have been walking around in a daze. A couple of weeks ago, I looked at myself in the mirror. I asked myself, when this began. When did I start back drinking like this? I realized that it was when my Daddy became sick and died. I have been depressed for a year and a half. As soon as I realized what was wrong, I felt a weight lift from my shoulders."

He missed his Daddy. He missed Daddy's love.

God is waiting for you to ask for His help to heal the wounds, destroy the holes, and bring you into wholeness. Let Him stop the bleeding. He is waiting with outstretched arms to stop the curse. He is our refuge and our defense.

In the fear of the Lord there is strong confidence, and His children will have refuge.
Proverbs 14:26 NLT

Daddy loves us so very much. There is no measure of His love. He wants to make us whole. He's waiting to bring us into right relationship and fellowship with Him. Daddy will never walk away, turning His back on His children. He desires to spend T-I-M-E with us.

Let your unfailing love surround us, LORD, for our hope is in You alone. Psalms 33:22 NLT

And now is the time when we put can put pride to the side. It's the time that we can be real with God. He already knows the hurt. He knows the secret things of our heart. He knows and understands the pain. He's ready to heal us, if we only ask. There is no failure in Him. He has the answers to the needs of your heart. Why don't you let Him make you whole today?

**O LORD, the earth is full of Your unfailing love; teach me Your principles.
Psalms 119:64 NLT**

Sometimes rather than risking failure, we refuse to try. Change can be risky and scary. If, I didn't try, I didn't fail. I actually succeeded in staying trapped in my comfort zone. However, there are so many things out there to brighten our world. Some of them are worth taking the risk. Let's expand our comfort zone. Let's risk bringing new ideas into the comfort zone. Remember that we may fall down, but we can get back up. If God is guiding, He is also providing. If He is leading, He is also proceeding. It's in Him that we have the victory.

The LORD is my strength and my song;
He has become my victory. He is my God,
and I will praise Him; He is my father's God,
and I will exalt Him! Exodus 15:2 NLT

And now the LORD speaks—He who formed me in my mother's womb to be His servant, who commissioned me to bring His people of Israel back to Him. The LORD has honored me, and my God has given me strength.
Isaiah 49:5

From the Heart of Charlotte

Recently, in what can only be described as an extreme leap of faith or an ultimate act of stupidity, I opened my life up to the public scrutiny of the world. After postponing writing *A Journey to Hell and Back* for a number of years, I began the agonizing process. It was not revisiting the events that caused my heart so much grief. It was knowing the prejudice and misconceptions that surround so many population groups. Revealing that the Good Samaritan had been apart of these populations caused me immense agony. Realizing that I had a charge bigger than myself, I defied my personal discomfort and wrote the book that today is bringing hope to so many people around the world.

"Lay down the knife," the angel said. "Do not hurt the boy in any way, for now I know that you truly fear God. You have not withheld even your beloved son from Me. "Then Abraham looked up and saw a ram caught by its horns in a bush. So he took the ram and sacrificed it as a burnt offering on the altar in place of his son. Abraham named the place

162

"The LORD Will Provide." This name has now become a proverb: "On the mountain of the LORD it will be provided. "Then the angel of the LORD called again to Abraham from heaven, "This is what the LORD says: Because you have obeyed Me and have not withheld even your beloved son, I swear by My own self that I will bless you richly. I will multiply your descendants into countless millions, like the stars of the sky and the sand on the seashore. They will conquer their enemies, and through your descendants, all the nations of the earth will be blessed—all because you have obeyed Me."
Genesis 22: 12-18 NLT

What did it cost me to write these books? Everything! I sacrificed my reputation, my career, and close relationships to be obedient to God. In my obedience, I risked losing the love and respect of my children and my husband. I risked becoming further alienated from other family members. Furthermore, I risked losing my car, house, and all the material possessions that I had acquired. That hurt. However, there was something that hurt me even more. I had worked so hard to make reparations for my actions. My educational achievements didn't come easy. My reputation at one point seemed beyond repair; yet, I had a new reputation. God had given me everything that I have. Now, as He did with Abraham and the son of promise, He asked me to sacrifice my reputation back to Him.

Many people have asked how I could open my life and failures up to the world. They have said that they would never have done what I did. The answers are very simple. God prepared me for the task. How could I not be obedient? What did I have to lose that God didn't give me? Absolutely nothing!!!!!!

My health may fail, and my spirit may grow weak, but God remains the strength of my heart; He is mine forever. Psalm 73:26NLT

Several years ago, I was given a message, *Where do you want to take Him.* God revealed to me just how much He knew about me. Many times, we are overly concerned about our parents learning our secrets. We are afraid that our friends will reject or demean us if they know the truth. God let me know that He is my real Daddy, and He is my real friend. He knows everything that I have ever done and ever will do and yet He loves me.

And here is how to measure it—the greatest love is shown when people lay down their lives for their friends.
John 15:13 NLT

It was for the Charlotte with all the shameful secrets that He sent His son to die in her place. It wasn't for the Charlotte with the good name or reputation. Real love is willing to sacrifice for the good of others, even unto death. He has promised never to leave me or forsake me. Daddy has been faithful to His word.

For God so loved the world that He gave His only Son, so that everyone who believes in Him will not perish but have eternal life.
John 3:16

I never wanted to write *A Journey to Hell and Back*. The book was delayed for more than eight years. It was only after my back was against the wall that I was obedient to God. For two weeks almost non-stop, I cried as I typed the story that would expose Charlotte Russell to the world. My grief was caused by the fact that I am no longer Charlotte Russell but Charlotte Johnson. For the first time in years, I felt the pain of being a Black Sheep. The poem *Black Sheep, Black Sheep* was my consolation straight from the throne of God.

Since we respect our earthly fathers who disciplined us, should we not all the more cheerfully submit to the discipline of our heavenly Father and live forever?
Hebrews 12:9 NLT

Did I think about how people would look at me? Did I think about how they would talk about me or judge me? Did I think that some people would misunderstand my motives and me? I thought about all of that. Did it happen? Yes, in some cases that has been exactly what happened. Am I sorry I wrote the book? Absolutely, not!

My priorities are in order. I realize that I don't have anything that God didn't first give me. If I live my entire life and God is not pleased with me, my living has been in vain. When it's all said and done, I want God to be pleased with me.

> The Lord is my light and my salvation—
> so why should I be afraid?
> The Lord protects me from danger—
> so why should I tremble.
> When evil people come to destroy me, when my enemies and foes attack me, they will stumble and fall. Though a mighty army surrounds me, my heart will know no fear. Even if they attack me, I remain confident. He will place me out of reach on a high rock.
> Then I will hold my head high, above my enemies who surround me. At his Tabernacle I will offer sacrifices with shouts of joy, singing and praising the Lord with music. Listen to my pleading, O Lord. Be merciful and answer me! My heart has heard you say, "Come and talk with me." And my heart responds, "Lord, I am coming." Do not hide yourself from me. Do not reject your servant in anger. You have always been my helper. Don't leave me now; don't abandon me, O God of my salvation! Even if my father and mother abandon me, the Lord

will hold me close. Teach me how to live, O Lord. Lead me along the path of honesty, for my enemies are waiting for me to fall. Do not let me fall into their hands. For they accuse me of things I've never done and breathe out violence against me.

Yet I am confident that I will see the Lord's goodness while I am here in the land of the living. Wait patiently for the Lord. Be brave and courageous. Yes, wait patiently for the Lord. Psalm 27:1-14 NLT

A psalm of David.

How has my life changed since writing the book? I was totally obedient, for probably the first time in my life. I offered a total living sacrifice to my Lord. It was an act of total trust, total faith. It was *Faith unto Grace* in action. It was truly believing that His grace is sufficient for me. It has been sufficient.

"For I know the plans I have for you," says the LORD. "They are plans for good and not for disaster, to give you a future and a hope." Jeremiah 29:11

My obedience has been rewarded in countless ways. I am totally in awe of God. I am completely amazed at His grace and His love. His plan for my life was bigger than anything that I ever dreamed or imagined could happen to me. Now, I ask you to trust

Him with that same kind of faith. Trust Him enough to be honest with Him. Be so honest with Him that it hurts. Surgery hurts. But sometimes we have to hurt to get better. Trust Him until it hurts. Trust Him until He makes you whole. Trust Him until He makes you complete. He's Daddy.

I have told you these things, so that in Me you may have peace. In this world you will have trouble. But take heart! I have overcome the world. John 16:33 NIV

Do for others as you would like them to do for you. Luke 6:31

Prologue

And, ye fathers, provoke not your children to wrath: but bring them up in the nurture and admonition of the Lord.
Ephesians 6:4

This book focused on the seriousness of fatherhood or more appropriately the seriousness of lacking a positive father figure. However, it is not meant to offer excuses for social, moral, economic, or spiritual failure. The Bible teaches that even nature testifies that there is a God. No one will ever stand in the presence of God and say, "I wanted to know you, but I had a bad father."

The soul that sinneth, it shall die. The son shall not bear the iniquity of the father, neither shall the father bear the iniquity of the son: the righteousness of the righteous shall be upon him, and the wickedness of the wicked shall be upon him. Ezekiel 18: 20

Parents must take the job of being parents seriously. Parenting is much more than merely fulfilling a biological imperative. The term father denotes fulfilling a biological function. However, being a Daddy means being concerned about every aspect of the child's growth and development. It means caring about where the child is and who his friends are. It means knowing the child's interests and encouraging right and proper ones. It also means discouraging, and even forbidding those interests and activities that are inappropriate or dangerous.

Today millions of children have single parents, most of which are female. Mothers were never meant to be good fathers. God created husband and wife because He knew each would serve particular roles. While some parents leave the home altogether, other parents blend into the woodwork. Credit must be given to the single parents who courageously carry on these additional responsibilities left by the absent parent. However, there is no way to make up for the nurturing potential of the absent parent.

It is sad commentary when men have children and never father them. They pass the responsibility on to the child's mother and neglect their responsibility. They work hard at not being involved. They ignore their children and spend their time engaging in other activities that they have deemed a priority. This neglect or abuse as it may be appropriately called can leave deep and lasting scars in the heart of the child.

Faithful, loving spiritual care from faithful Christian mothers, especially those mothers whose husbands have abandoned their families, is an enormous asset and blessing to their families. Let us thank and praise God for faithful mothers, who, like Timothy's mother, Eunice and grandmother, Lois nurtured their children with the Word of God, leading them to know the grace and mercy of our Lord and Savior Jesus Christ.

The Bible speaks on this subject in the book of Proverbs. It records this oracle given to King Lemuel by his mother:

> **Strength and dignity are her clothing, and she smiles at the future. She opens her mouth in wisdom, and the teaching of kindness is on her tongue. She looks well to the ways of her household, and does not eat the bread of idleness. Her children rise up and bless her...charm is deceitful and beauty is in vain, but a woman who fears the Lord, she shall be praised. Give her the fruit of her hands, and let her works praise her in the gates Proverbs 31:25-31**

When God's intention for the family is broken through the sinful actions on the part of human beings, this does not void His will for the family. He has a perfect will. Those who walk in His 'permissive will' have really walked out of His will. He knows what's best for His children. However, He will support and strengthen faithful women of God who must assume the leadership of their family that their husband abandoned.

The position and authority of the father as the head of the family are expressly assumed and sanctioned in Scripture, as a likeness of that of the Almighty over His creatures. This position of authority was obviously at the root of the patriarchal form of government. The father's blessings were regarded as conferring special benefit, but his damnation proclaimed special injury, on those upon whom it fell.

> **Then Noah said, "May Shem be blessed by the Lord my God; and may Canaan be his servant. May God enlarge the territory of Japheth, and may he share the prosperity of Shem; and let Canaan be his servant." Genesis 9:26-27 NLT**

While he was still a long way off, his father saw him, and felt compassion for him, and ran and embraced him, and kissed him.
Luke 15:20

The Bible presents the scenario of godly sons and ungodly fathers throughout the Old and New Testament. If the children were only products of parental influence, the children would bare no responsibility for their own actions as adults. The parents would shoulder total responsibility for the outcome of their children's lives. However, the Bible presents children as responsible and answering for themselves and their own sins.

A wise son heareth his father's instruction: but a scorner heareth not rebuke. Prov. 13:1

Asa was Judah's first righteous king. The amazing thing is that Asa was so godly while his father, Abijam, was so wicked. There are numerous other Biblical examples of these godly and ungodly relationships.

And Abijam slept with his fathers; and they buried him in the city of David: and Asa his son reigned in his stead. And Asa did that which was right in the eyes of the Lord, as did David his father.
I Kgs. 15: 8, 11

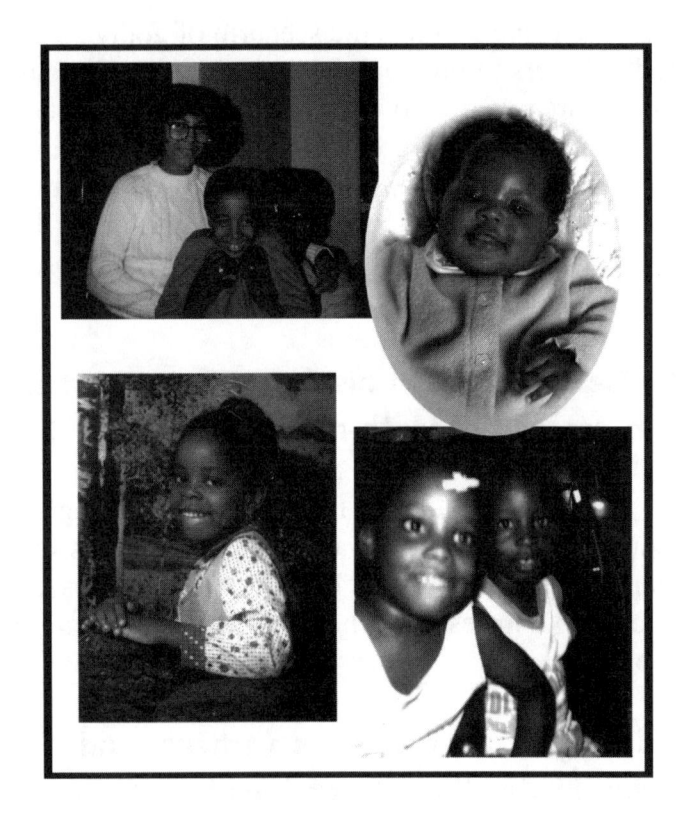

When everything else is said and done remember to give your Children Daddy's hugs, Daddy's kisses, and Daddy's love...